S0-CTA-837

FINDING GOD'S VISION: MISSIONS AND THE NEW REALITIES

William Tinsley

Scripture taken from the NEW AMERICAN STANDARD BIBLE, ©
1960, 1962, 1963, 1968, 1971, 1972, 1973, 1975, 1977, by The
Lockman Foundation. Used by permission.

© 2005 by William Tinsley
second printing August 2005

Published by Veritas Publishing
303 Rockbrook
Rockwall, Texas 75087

Printed in the United States of America

All rights are reserved. No part of this publication may be reproduced,
stored in a retrieval system or transmitted in any form or by any means
– for example, electronic, photocopy, recording – without the prior
written permission of the publisher. The only exception is brief
quotations in printed reviews.

Cover Design by The Manning Group, Dallas, Texas
Debbie Sheppard, Designer

Tinsley, William, 2005
   Finding God's Vision: Missions and the New Realities

ISBN 0-9708118-6-1

To order additional copies go to www.veritaspublish.com

TABLE OF CONTENTS

INTRODUCTION

After having been on the journey for a long time, I offer this book as one who is discovering open doors that lead to unimaginable opportunity for the future of missions. My prayer is that this book will be useful in stimulating the minds of leaders in our churches to explore new possibilities for missions. Undoubtedly, if they do, they will discover God's activity in our day in terms that can only be defined as "miraculous."

I also pray for those who are already "on the journey" with God into the missions paradigms of the twenty-first century that they will find clarification and encouragement. They are not alone. Many others are exploring and experiencing missions in terms the world has not known since the first century.

As you read through these pages, you will discover that the seven new realities are interrelated. They weave together reinforcing one another like threads in a tapestry. They are more organic than mechanical. None of these new realities alone could create the profound changes that reshape the world and redefine the means of accomplishing the Great Commission of Christ.

God's vision is the indispensable element that breathes life and purpose into the new realities. Without God's vision, we are left struggling on the shores of a sea of change. I pray for everyone who reads these pages that they will become capture by God's vision for their life.

Journeys with God are never easy. My path to the present era of unprecedented movements of God's spirit worldwide went through some very dark canyons. I can remember the painful day when the only song that resonated with my experience was "I will worship you."

I will worship you in the midnight hour,
I will worship you when I'm in the fire,
I will worship you when the night seems long,
I will worship you when all hope seems gone,
I will worship you.

I never stopped worshiping God and seeking him. I am grateful He surprised me with the growing discovery of his activity in His people, His churches and the nations of the earth. I am grateful for those who have helped me along the journey. I am grateful for my colleagues at WorldconneX who continue to stretch me in areas I have not known. And, as always, I am deeply grateful to my family, my wife, my sons, my daughter and my grandchildren who fill my life with joy.

Special acknowledgement is due to Carol Childress and David Williams who offered invaluable advice and editorial assistance to bring this manuscript to its final form. Any errors or shortcomings, of course, are my own. But they have made the final form far better than it would have been without them, just as they have helped make me a better person through their friendship.

As you read these pages, I pray God will give you a taste or a glimpse of what He is doing in your life so that you will be awakened to join God in His mysterious journey to redeem the world to Himself through Jesus Christ.

CHAPTER ONE

A DIFFERENT WORLD

Human history flows like the waters of a river. It starts with small streams that converge into a larger current. At times the movement is slow and languid. At other times change comes rapidly like waterfalls cascading over rocks and twisting through canyons with irresistible power.

We are living in one of those white water periods. Like rafters, we feel out of control, threatened and confused. We feel powerless to chart a course and can only react to the shifting current, trying to avoid the next boulder, attempting to catch the surge of power that will catapult us forward.

Our only sense of safety and security in times such as this comes from God. God is Lord of history, and the Bible shows how He worked in and through history from the creation of the world through the first century A.D. Clearly, He was in charge and used people, circumstances, natural forces and even the rise and fall of kingdoms for His purposes.

But what about the two thousand years since the close of the New Testament? Did God cease his activity? Did God leave the remainder of human history up to random chance and human decisions? Where does the dawn of the twenty-first century fit into God's redemptive work? What is God doing in the world and the church today?

When God established the church, he gave all of His Word and all of his work to all of his people to reach all of the nations. But, through the centuries, both the Word of God and

1

the work of God were removed from the people of God. During the Reformation of the sixteenth century God returned His Word to His people. Today, God is restoring His work to His people.

To better understand this, we will take a quick look at three pivotal eras of history: the First Century, the Reformation, and today.

The First Century

The Bible describes the focal point of all human history with these words: "In the fullness of time, God sent forth His son, born of a virgin, born under the law." The birth of Jesus was a remarkable moment, culminating hundreds of years of religious, secular and cultural development that made this time "ripe" for the intervention of God.

Jesus was born when the *pax Romana*, the peace of Rome, had spread across the Mediterranean world. Along with Roman domination came roads, travel, trade and the *lingua franca*, Greek, the language of commerce that would transcend ancient provincial barriers between nations. For Roman citizens, like Paul, the Roman law afforded protection for personal safety and justice. From any of the obscure districts and regions of the Empire, a Roman citizen could appeal to the law of Rome, as Paul did at Philippi and again in Caesarea.

Common men and women carried the gospel into every corner of the Roman Empire, often meeting in homes, often persecuted. These were not "professionals." When Paul instructed his young protégés, Timothy and Titus on the qualifications that distinguish a potential leader in the church, he gave very practical advice. Look for those who have demonstrated good people skills in their homes, in their church and in the world. Look for those with

2

sound doctrine, spiritual maturity and moral integrity. His instructions are noticeably void of any formal theological training with diplomas or certificates. These were irrelevant. They did not exist. The potential leaders were already in the churches that were planted. They were already respected leaders in their homes and their communities. (1 Timothy 3:2-12; Titus 1:5-9).

The Reformation

In 312 AD the Roman Emperor Constantine gave Christianity favored status in his empire and placed the symbol of the cross on the shields of his army as divine protection. This decision by the emperor began a radical transformation of the once persecuted faith.

Ornate cathedrals were constructed at great expense to the empire. A hierarchy of bishops and priests began to occupy positions of sacred and secular influence. Constantine ousted the polytheistic gods of the pantheon and replaced them with Christianity. As the ruler of Rome, Constantine remained the ruler of religion and sat in judgment at the Council of Nicea to rule on matters of theology.

As Rome spread westward through Europe, and as the church advanced in its influence to the point that the Pope could crown the Emperor, citizenship became synonymous with Christianity. Infant baptism carried with it the sacramental significance of both secular and spiritual citizenship.

As part of this process, the people of God lost touch with the Word of God. Only the clergy, popes, bishops, priests and monks had access to the Scripture, and that only in Greek and Latin. The people of God could not read the Bible for themselves. They were considered incapable of comprehending and interpreting its mysteries. Only the clergy could study Scripture and give interpretation.

At the same time, the people of God lost touch with the work of God. The state paid the clergy to carry out the work of the church by levying taxes on the entire populace since they were all considered members of the church as citizens of the state. The people of God were obligated only to be good citizens, which meant paying taxes, doing their labor, raising their families, serving in the military and obeying government and church officials.

There were notable exceptions, counter movements of spiritual vitality that formed like eddies along the edge of the great river. Chrysostom (347-407), Augustine (354-430), Patrick of Ireland (387-461), Bernard of Clairveaux (1091-1153), John Tauler (1300-1361) and Savanarola (1452-1498) are a few.

Of course, God was not willing that His Word and His work should always be withheld from His people. In the fifteenth and sixteenth centuries God initiated the return of His Word to His people through two disconnected and obscure individuals.

Johann Gutenberg was born about 1400 in Mainz, Germany. Except for his numerous legal conflicts (most related to his struggles to make a living in Mainz and Strassburg) we would know almost nothing about his life, other than the fact that his efforts to make money motivated him to invent the first printing press. That Gutenberg was no spiritual giant moved by inspiration to advance God's kingdom is evidenced by the fact that he first invented a process to polish mirrors so that religious pilgrims could capture the reflections of relics and hence store their power. Before using his printing press to produce copies of the Bible, he first printed indulgences, certificates sold by the Catholic Church that promised to release relatives from Purgatory while funding the construction of St. Peter's Cathedral in Rome.

Nonetheless, his printing press paved the way for the Reformation. Its influence on civilization was second only to the invention of writing as a process by which information could be stored and shared across generations. Up until Gutenberg, all copies of written material were laboriously produced by hand

Johann Gutenberg's introduction of the printing press in 1455 set the stage for a communications revolution that would leave little untouched. Documents that were previously painstakingly copied by hand were now mass produced in comparatively large quantities. It is not coincidental that the period we know as the Renaissance and the Reformation followed soon on the heels of Gutenberg's invention.

Brilliant minds converged like rare stars aligned in the night sky. Leonardo DaVinci (1469-1536) explored the possibilities of flight with his mechanical sketches and left anatomical drawings and art that still stagger the imagination. Christopher Columbus successfully enlisted the support of the Queen of Spain for his voyage beyond the edge of the known world in 1492. Magellan successfully launched the first attempt to sail around the world in 1519, a feat completed by his crew in 1521. Copernicus revolutionized all understanding of the universe in 1543 with his hypothesis that the sun was the center of the solar system with the earth and other planets orbiting around it.

In the middle of these events, God raised up a tormented young monk named Martin Luther. Born in Eisleben Germany in 1483 and destined for law school by his father, Luther vowed to become a monk when faced with his own death in a thunder storm in 1505. The terrors of hell drove him to the monastery and long hours of confession. His world was transformed as a young theologian studying the Greek New Testament when he hit upon the revelation that God's righteousness is bestowed by grace through faith in Jesus Christ. Romans 1:17 changed his life: "For in it the righteousness of God is revealed from faith to faith; as it is written, 'The one who is righteous will live by faith.'"

Martin Luther's protest of the excesses and erroneous teachings of the Catholic Church in 1517 launched the Reformation. He would soon translate the Scriptures into German. Other reformers would follow such as John Calvin, Ulrich Zwingli and John Knox.

Within a relatively narrow window of time, the world changed. On the one hand the foundations for scientific investigation and the industrial revolution were laid. On the other, God gave his Word back to his people. No longer was the Bible the province of clergy and the church. Men and women of all ages could read the Bible for themselves. It was to this end, to promote literacy to read the Bible, that many of the educational institutions of the last four centuries were established.

For the last four hundred years, we have been riding the crest of the Reformation wave. In its wake, denominations sprang up and multiplied. The common current that drove most denominations was the passion to preach, teach and practice the Word of God.

The Twenty-first Century

Although the Word of God was given back to God's people in the Reformation, the work of God remained with the clergy. The clergy reserved the provinces of preaching and administering the ordinances.

As denominations settled into mainline practices, the gap between clergy and laity remained intact. Missions remained the province of the professional missionary who was supported by denominational agencies to carry the gospel to pagan lands beyond the Christian "empire" as we knew it. The people remained in their place. The average Christian was to be a faithful church member, give to support the church budget and the special missions offerings and pray for those who were "called" to represent them as missionaries in foreign lands. They were, as the saying went, to "hold the ropes."

There were notable exceptions, especially among Baptists and Methodists on the western frontier where there were few seminary trained clergy. Bi-vocational and lay preachers had to take up the task. Where this occurred, the gospel spread rapidly and churches multiplied.

We are at another pivotal point of history. God is restoring all of His work to all of His people to reach all of the nations. In the remaining chapters, we will explore seven new realities that God is using to re-write, re-wire and re-configure His work among the nations. These new realities are:

- A Connected World
- Global Business
- Population Migration
- A New Center of Christianity
- The Emergence of New Missions Organizations
- Churches to the Forefront of Missions
- Returning God's Work to the Laity

Before we examine each of these new realities, we will focus on finding God's vision. That is the key to the future. God has a vision for every person and every church and He wants every believer to live a significant life with eternal importance. Once we have examined how you can find God's vision, we will then consider each of the new realities to discover how God's vision can be fulfilled in the world today.

Questions for Reflection and Discussion

1. Identify and list the ways the world has changed in your lifetime.

2. How are corporations conducting business differently than they were twenty years ago?

3. What are the implications for how missions can be done differently today?

CHAPTER TWO

FINDING GOD'S VISION

Fifty days after Jesus' crucifixion, Peter stood in a chaotic whirl-wind of people. According to the Bible, those gathered in Jerusalem were "Parthians and Medes and Elamites, and residents of Mesopotamia, Judea and Cappadocia, Pontus and Asia, Phrygia and Pamphylia, Egypt and the districts of Libya around Cyrene, and visitors from Rome, both Jews and proselytes, Cretans and Arabs ..." (Acts 2:9-11). They were all hearing the gospel of Jesus Christ for the first time. It could have been a scene out of the twenty-first century. The setting was cosmopolitan, multi-ethnic, multi-cultural and multi-lingual.

Peter reached back to the prophet Joel for explanations about what was happening: "'And it shall be in the last days,' God says, 'that I will pour forth of My spirit upon all mankind; and your sons and your daughters shall prophesy, and your young men shall see visions, and your old men shall dream dreams; even upon my bond slaves both men and women, I will in those days pour forth of My spirit and they shall prophesy.'" (Acts 2:17-18).

This is precisely what is happening in the twenty-first century. God is pouring out his Spirit. He is creating movements among the nations and He is using the young and old, both men and women, to do it. The driving force behind what God is doing in the world is visions and dreams.

In almost forty years of ministry, I have discovered that relatively few Christians and even fewer churches have discovered God's vision for their life. Most Christians and most churches are extremely busy and doing many good things, including giving to missions, going on mission trips and carrying out the programs of the church. But those who discover God's vision experience something unique. They are transformed. They discover a quality of life that goes far beyond "doing church," or "doing missions." I am convinced that many believers and churches today are hungry for God's vision. But most don't know how to find it.

We must understand what God's vision is not.

The term "vision" is widely used and does not mean the same thing in every context.

1. God's Vision is not simply "Visioning."

Visioning is used in sports as a means to achieve successful performance in competition. It conjures up images of Tiger Woods, Vijay Singh or Phil Mickelson stalking the green, examining the contour and curve, standing behind their ball and "visioning" the exact path and speed of their putt to the hole before stepping up to hit. They follow much the same pattern on the tee, in the fairway and the rough. Every successful golfer "visions" the flight of the ball before he hits it. Jack Nicklaus once said, "I never hit a shot, not even in practice, without having a sharp in-focus picture of it in my head."

Baseball pitchers "vision" each pitch before they throw. Tennis players "vision" each serve and each shot. Football players "vision" the game including their opponents and each play before they ever suit up.

Visioning is used in business planning for corporations, both profit and non-profit. A common practice to establish goals, priorities and strategies for the future is to first "vision" the future. Where do you want to go? What do you want to accomplish? What could the corporation look like in five years, fifteen or twenty? First comes the "visioning," then the planning. Entire consulting services have been created to provide "visioning" resources for management. They offer their consultant services to organizations, corporations, communities and churches.

All of these "visioning" disciplines are good. They recognize essential steps any person or organization must take to accomplish a desired outcome or to move forward to a desired future. But, this is not what we mean when we talk about "finding God's vision."

2, God's Vision is not simply vision casting

Virtually every book written on leadership emphasizes the importance of casting vision. It is how leaders lead. But most effective leaders have not simply read a book on vision casting and decided on a vision that will compel people to follow. Most effective leaders cast vision because they are first captured by a compelling vision to such an extent they could not do otherwise.

This cannot be reduced to mere mechanics in a step by step manual. If it were that simple the world would be filled with leaders who are casting vision. Finding a vision so compelling that you cannot help but cast that vision to others is a far more intangible, intuitive and emotional experience. It takes place somewhere in the soul and often resides in the deep places, not on the surface.

Vision is powerful. No leader is able to effectively lead without it. And no leader with vision can lead without casting vision.

Abraham Lincoln was casting vision when he stepped to the platform at Gettysburg and delivered his two-minute speech that still inspires generations a century and a half since he spoke. Do you think that Lincoln consciously thought about casting his vision on that occasion? I doubt it. Within the words of his brief speech he said, "The world will little note what we say here." Lincoln was able to cast a vision that transcended time, place and circumstance because he was captured by that vision.

Martin Luther King, Jr. was casting vision when he stood on the steps of the Lincoln Memorial in 1963 and announced "I have a dream!" Dr. King was probably more aware of the significant moment of responsibility than Lincoln was when he stood in the obscure hills of Pennsylvania. After all, Dr. King was speaking to a crowd of 250,000 people and he knew his speech would be instantaneously televised to the nation. We still have access to those televised recordings. Visit any number of web sites and you can both hear and see the "I Have a Dream" speech delivered by Dr. King. You will likely be gripped by his passion. Dr. King's sermon was compelling because Dr. King was compelled. The dream was in his soul.

Vision casting, in and of itself, is not the same as finding God's vision. It is only a tool to be used after finding God's vision.

3. God's vision is not simply a vision statement.

Vision statements are good. They help to clarify where an organization is going, where we want to come out at the end, what we want to accomplish. They can pull us together to share energy and resources in the pursuit of a common goal.

Almost all organizations today, and many individuals, have a vision statement. Whether it is the National Center for Bicycling and Walking or the Department of Homeland Security, every organization seems to have a vision statement.

The process of finding a vision statement usually goes something like this. A group meets together and brainstorms words or phrases relating to vision, mission and values. These are then grouped into the three categories. The words and phrases relating to vision are then matched and compared until a composite vision statement begins to emerge. Once drafted the statement is presented to "stakeholders" for comment, feedback and consensus.

12

The final version becomes the vision statement for the organization. The process is periodically repeated.

As good and helpful as this process might be for any organization, it does not necessary bring us to God's vision. Many churches have adopted vision statements, but there is no inner or outward indication that the church is captivated by a compelling vision from God that is transforming their lives, their community and the world.

Finding God's vision must be more than doing what every corporation and institution does. We must go beyond visualizing, casting vision and writing vision statements. How do we do this?

We must understand what God's vision is.

God's vision comes from God. This may sound overly simplistic or obvious, but the fact of the matter is that most of the "visioning" processes created by the corporate world and adopted by our churches are designed to discover vision that comes from us. The question most often asked in the process is, "What is your vision?" It is not, "What is God's vision?" Finding God's vision is something entirely different than finding our vision. God's vision comes from outside of us, captures us and compels us to go places and do things we would never have done on our own. This is why Paul states to King Agrippa, "I did not prove disobedient to the heavenly vision."

Paul was destined on a radically different course until he met Jesus on the road to Damascus. He was firmly and violently opposed to anything related to the followers of Christ. But in that moment he met God in a vision and his life was completely changed. The vision did not come from within Paul. He did not sit down and work it out. The vision came from outside of him. The vision came from God.

This is not to imply that Paul instantly had all the answers. It would, in fact, take him a long time to figure out the implications of that moment in which he encountered Jesus. The words spoken to him in the vision of Christ would not have full meaning until many years had passed. By his own account he spent a long period of time in Arabia and waited three years before going up to Jerusalem to meet "Cephas" and the leaders of the church (Galatians 1:17-18). After that he remained in Tarsus for some time before Barnabas brought him to Antioch where he spent a year leading Bible studies before being sent out with Barnabas on the first missionary journey.

But, at the point of his initial vision on the Damascus road, Paul started on a journey of discovery. The compelling force that would drive him was no longer rooted in his own desires and ambitions. From this point forward he was captured and compelled by God's vision.

Of course few of us ever experience a vision like Paul's vision on the Damascus road. This may be one reason he referred to this experience so seldom. Perhaps he knew that a blinding light and an audible voice was not the norm for every believer. But there are clues in Paul's experience that will help you discover God's vision for your life and God's vision for your church.

What gripped Paul about the vision was not the phenomenon, but the content. "For this purpose I have appeared to you, to appoint you a minister and a witness not only to the things which you have seen, but also to the things in which I will appear to you; delivering you from the Jewish people and from the Gentiles, to whom I am sending you, to open their eyes so that they may turn from darkness to light and from the dominion of Satan to God, that they may receive forgiveness of sins and an inheritance among those who have been sanctified by faith in Me." (Act 26:16-18).

You might say that this was Paul's mission statement. But it was not a statement he created. It was the vision God gave him. It has general parameters that must be worked out on a daily basis in specific terms. God's vision for Paul is to make him an instrument for delivering people, especially Gentiles, from darkness to light, so that their sins are forgiven and they receive an inheritance in Heaven. The bright light and the audible voice are incidental to this vision.

God's vision comes in many ways to His people. Sometimes His vision comes in a quiet whisper as it did for Heather when God whispered to her: "India." She became convinced God wanted her to work among the handicapped in India. Sometimes His vision comes over many years as it did for Steve. When I was in Guatemala I met Steve who works with orphans through Buckner Orphan Care International. I was fascinated by Steve's story. In the 1970s Steve was a wealthy young entrepreneur sharing in the success of Silicon Valley in California. He was a nominal Christian caught up in the competitive rat race to succeed. As his wealth increased, so did his dissatisfaction with life. He was miserable. His marriage failed. About that time, he read the story of the Rich Young Ruler and considered Jesus' words: "sell all you have and give it to the poor, and come, take up your cross and follow me." He decided to take Jesus at his word, sold everything he had and gave it to the poor and set out on a new course to follow Jesus wherever it took him. Over a period of years, Steve found God's vision relieving poverty and neglect among the children of Guatemala. I have met few people in my life who radiate greater joy.

How can I find God's Vision?

Embrace a vital relationship with Jesus Christ through repentance and faith.

You cannot find God's vision for your life or your church without a relationship of faith with Jesus Christ. This is why Jesus came

15

preaching repentance. It is impossible to have a relationship with God and find His vision unless we repent. Matthew tells us this was at the core of Jesus' message. He says, "From that time Jesus began to preach and say, 'Repent for the kingdom of God is at hand.'" (Matthew 4:17). And again, Jesus said, "Unless you repent, you will all likewise perish." (Luke 13:3-5). The word "repent" has almost dropped out of our Christian vocabulary. Few preachers preach about repentance. Fewer people, still, understand it. This might be why we see so many churches that are impotent when it comes to transforming their community. Too often churches are riddled with immorality, filled with people who harbor grudges, resentment, anger and suspicion. Such churches cannot possibly find God's vision.

At its simplest level, repentance is turning from any known sin in our life and mending any broken relationship. We cannot expect to find God's vision if we are harboring secret sins we are unwilling to give up or if we are living in broken relationships that need to be mended.

At its highest level, repentance is a transformation of the mind. This is the root meaning of the word *metanoia*. *Meta* means "change" or "transform" and *nous* means "mind." When we experience repentance our core values are transformed from the values of this world to the values of His kingdom. This is what Paul meant when he said, "Be not conformed to this world, but be transformed by the renewing of your minds." As long as our values are the same as those of everyone else in the world we will not find God's vision.

Listen to Scripture

God's vision will always be in harmony with Scripture. Search the Scriptures until you are captivated by the heart of God. Listen to the larger themes: God's redemptive work in the world beginning with creation, continuing with the call of Abraham as a blessing to

16

the nations and culminating in Jesus Christ. Study the Sermon on the Mount. Memorize it. Meditate on it. Live it.

When Jesus introduced his ministry, he reached back to the prophet Isaiah: "The Spirit of the Lord is upon me because he anointed me to preach the gospel to the poor. He has sent me to proclaim release to the captives, and recovery of sight to the blind, to set free those who are oppressed, to proclaim the favorable year of the Lord." (Luke 4:17-19; Isaiah 61:1-2). In some ways, this was God's vision statement for Jesus. Whatever God's vision is for you, it will be in harmony with the work of Jesus.

Listen to other believers

God speaks to us through other believers. Many times, across the years, I have observed common themes emerging in the body of Christ from sources unrelated to one another. When the Holy Spirit speaks His message is reinforced.

This was true for Paul. Shortly after his encounter with Jesus on the open road he received a visit from a believer he had never met. God spoke to Ananias in a vision and convinced him to pay a visit to Saul of Tarsus, the well-known persecutor of those who followed Jesus. At the same time, God confirmed to Paul that he would receive a visit from this humble but courageous believer. When they met, Ananias confirmed to Paul the fact that he was a chosen instrument to bear witness to the Gentiles, Kings and the sons of Israel. Paul needed this confirmation. He needed the personal touch of a fellow believer. So do you.

Listen to what others are saying regarding the way God has gifted you and the plans God has for you. You will hear common themes that reinforce one another. A picture will begin to take shape in your mind and heart regarding what God wants you to do.

Listen to your heart

Ultimately, you must listen to your heart. No one else can tell you what God's vision is for you. Finding God's vision is kind of like falling in love. You will know it when you see it and feel it.

Here is a clue: Finding God's vision is about experiencing God's pleasure.

Although I experienced this early in my journey with Christ, I only realized its power late in life. This was the theme of Jesus' ministry on this earth: he was always experiencing and doing the Father's pleasure. Isaiah 53:10 gives keen insight into the life and ministry of Jesus. Isaiah wrote, "Declaring the end from the beginning, and from ancient times, things which have not been done, saying, 'My purpose will be established, and I will accomplish all my good pleasure." (Isaiah 46:10). And again, "But the Lord was pleased to crush Him, putting Him to grief; if He would render Himself as a guilt offering, He will see his offspring, He will prolong His days, and the good pleasure of the Lord will prosper in His hand." (Isaiah 53:10). The words God spoke at Jesus' baptism could be translated: "You are my beloved son in whom I take great pleasure."

I have long been impressed with a scene from the movie, "Chariots of Fire" that tells the true story of Eric Liddle, the 1924 Olympic gold medal runner from Scotland. In that movie, Eric stands in a beautiful Sottish meadow with his cousin Jennie who is trying to persuade him to give up his running and go to China to fulfill his missionary calling. He turns to Jennie and says very gently, "Jennie, I believe God made me for a purpose, and he made me fast. When I run I feel his pleasure." Eric went on to win a gold medal in the 400 hundred meter dash, an event for which he had not trained. His pursuit of God's pleasure later took him to China where he died in a Japanese occupation camp as a witness to Christ.

Where do you feel God's pleasure?   What is God saying in your heart?

How can our church find God's Vision?

Focus on God

Aren't all churches focused on God? Unfortunately the answer is no. It is all too easy for churches to focus on themselves, their internal organization, their buildings, or the good things they do for God. Too often churches focus on survival trying to attract new members to help pay the bills.

To focus on God, a church must get beyond survival or even growth questions. God and his glory become the church's passion.

Cottonwood Baptist Church near Dublin, Texas discovered this truth. To visit Cottonwood Baptist Church, take Highway 377 from Fort Worth to Dublin. Turn left on Highway 6 at the only traffic light in town. About five miles outside Dublin, you will find Cottonwood Baptist church nestled under a grove of live oak trees on the left side of the road. The shade from the trees falls on wood frame buildings surrounded by a gravel parking lot. Most of the vehicles parked around the church are pickups. The air is heavy with the smell of cattle.

The pastor came to the church twenty years ago as a seminary student in his twenties. The church averaged twenty-five. He assumed this would be a seminary pastorate. He would stay a few years and move on to a larger church. But he became convinced that God's vision was for him to stay. He did. Across the years he led the church to focus on two things: the glory of God and authentic community. After fifteen years the church had grown to two-hundred and fifty, quite significant for an open country church in west Texas.

19

Five years ago, the church conducted a missions conference. Something unusual happened at that conference. The core values of the church, shaped around God's glory and authentic community connected with God's glory for the nations. The church was captured by God's vision, a larger vision than they had ever imagined.

Since that time the church has sent four families to China and adopted the Tarahumara, a native Indian people group in northwest Mexico. And the attendance has mushroomed from two-hundred fifty to nine hundred. Recently Cottonwood celebrated the pastor's twentieth anniversary. In an interview with the congregation, the pastor was asked, "What is your vision for the church?" His answer: "I envision the day our church will be sending out one hundred families throughout the world."

If you were to ask the pastor or the people how they grew such a dynamic church in the open country they would have difficulty answering. It is not a question they have entertained. Growth was never part of the equation. The swelling attendance came as a by-product, not as an end or goal that they pursued. They focused on God.

The church still looks like an open country church. If you drive by, there is nothing about the church that will catch your eye. The little wood frame building still stands out near the road in the shadow of live oak trees. They have built pre-fab buildings in the back to handle the crowd and they have spread more gravel so that the pick-up trucks won't get stuck on a rainy day.

Focus on prayer

I have attended thousands of "prayer meetings" in my life. And, all too often what passes for prayer in our churches has little to do with connecting with God.

In most cases, when our churches gather for prayer, we spend most of the time reporting on our illnesses: gall bladders, tumors, cancer, various illness and ailments. I have often been amazed at the gruesome detail with which some of these are described. To this we add our difficulties: unemployment, our need to sell or buy a house and various stresses. Then, once all of these have been duly collected, someone leads in a brief prayer to God that may or may not have anything to do with the litany of requests just noted.

But what is there about this kind of praying that is any different than the prayers of those who don't attend church? George Barna reports that 85% of Americans pray weekly. Most people pray regarding their own personal concerns: health, family, finances. This is not to say that we should not pray for such things. Nor is it to imply that God does not answer these prayers. After all, Jesus taught us to pray, "Give us this day our daily bread." But such prayer falls short of connecting with God's vision.

Prayer is about connecting and communicating with God. This can seldom be done effectively in a short span of time or in the hard rush of life. Certainly we ought to pray "on the go." But we must find times of solitude and quiet where we can focus and listen. That is why Jesus spent forty days in the wilderness. That is why Jesus often rose while it was still dark and went out to a solitary place to pray. (Mark 1:35). Jesus taught us to pray: "Thy kingdom come, thy will be done on earth as it is in Heaven." The focus of Jesus' prayer was always God's vision. That is why Jesus got alone the night before his crucifixion in order to pray, "Not my will but thy will be done." (Matthew 26:36-45).

Participate in a short term mission trip

Nothing will enlarge your vision for God's work in the world like personal experience and exposure in another country and another culture. Today there are any number of organizations that will include you in short term mission work all around the world. If

your church is a member of a denomination, contact your denominational offices for international volunteer missions opportunities.
Seek out other churches that are sending out volunteer teams and
join them.

Don't let the cost of international volunteer missions stop you
from going. Sometimes the decision is one of priority. Most of us
have more resources than we think. I once sold a car to raise the
funds for my fourteen year old son to go on an international
mission trip. If God is calling you to go, often family and friends
will help. I have never met anyone who regretted investing in an
international missions experience.

Take an "inventory" of your members

Listen to what God is saying in the lives of the people who are in
your church. What are their professions? What are their passions?
Where are their international connections? Every church is
unique. What makes each church unique are the lives of the
people who are in that church. This is exactly the way the church
at Antioch found God's vision in the first century. They listened to
what God was saying in the lives of their members and they heard
God's voice, "Set apart for Me Barnabas and Saul for the work to
which I have called them." (Acts 13:2). Keep this principle in mind
as you read the following chapters.

Become strategic

What if your church were a missionary? What would it look like?
Of course, your church is a missionary. God has given every
church and every Christian the Great Commandment and the
Great Commission. Northwood Church in Keller asked itself that
question and came up with some transforming answers.

If your church is a missionary, you will commit yourself to a
particular nation, people group and place. Most churches that

22

move to the front line of missions to engage the world usually adopt more than one nation, people group and place. But one is a great place to start.

All of this means that missions for your church must be strategic. Churches should not choose a particular place for missions investment based on convenience. This is no vacation. When I was Executive Director for Minnesota-Wisconsin Baptist Convention we were given two options for volunteer missions. One was to the Caribbean, a pretty nice place for Minnesotans who struggle through long winters of sub-zero temperatures. But our people said, "We want to go where other people don't want to go. We want to make a difference." So, we chose Siberia. It seemed like a good fit.

Remember that your missions involvement is not about you. The determining factor is not, "Will it be convenient and safe?" The real determining factor is, "Is this strategic to the Kingdom? Does God want us to go here?"

To find the answer to these final questions, your church might want to employ the services of a missions consultant. For many years churches have employed consultants for financial development, construction projects and growth campaigns. Why not employ a mission mentor who can coach the church to take the next step in finding God's vision to embrace the world?

Study what God is doing in the earth

God's vision has always included the nations of the earth. When He began his redemptive work in Abraham, he gave him the promise: "in your seed all the nations of the earth shall be blessed." (Genesis 22:18). When Jesus gave the Great Commission, he commanded His followers to "Make disciples of all the nations." (Matthew 28:19). The word used in the New Testament for "nations" is *ethne*. It is sometimes translated in our English

23

Bibles as "Gentiles." It is the root word of our term, "ethnic" or "ethnicity." It is the same word Paul used in Colossians 1:27 when he explained God's mystery that has been hidden in the past but that God is now making known among the *ethne*.

God's vision must be bigger than just growing our churches, building our buildings, paving our parking lots, implementing the latest program. God's vision always extends to the peoples of the earth. His ultimate purpose and vision is reflected in Revelation 7:9. "I looked, and behold, a great multitude which no one could count, from every nation and all tribes and peoples and tongues, standing before the throne and before the Lamb, clothed in white robes." We must be willing to let God take us into new and unfamiliar territory if we are to embrace His vision.

Most of us live rather provincial lives. In spite of the flood of international news through radio, television, the Internet and newspapers, we have a way of insulating our worlds. We like the comfort of the familiar. But to find God's vision, we must expose ourselves to the unfamiliar.

A few years ago one of my colleagues took us on a "field trip" to visit a Hari Krishna temple only blocks away from the building in which we worked in downtown Dallas. I sat there listening to the Hari Krishna priest explain his religion. I watched the elderly and the young wander into the temple that reeked of incense. They bowed upon their knees and offered sacrifices to the Krishna gods. It gave me chills.

Sometimes the world God wants us to reach is only blocks off our beaten paths. Take a new look at your community. Visit Buddhist temples, Islamic mosques. Drive through ethnic neighborhoods. Look for ethnic shops, stores and restaurants. Watch the children playing in the neighborhoods.

The book, *Operation World* contains demographic and religious information along with prayer requests for virtually every country and people group in the world. I have used it for personal devotionals to pray for nations and peoples around the globe. It is a great resource for personal or group prayer for missions. Find ways to expose your church to information about the spiritual and physical needs in other nations.

Almost every church today will have members who are traveling internationally with their companies. Help them see their travels as more than circumstantial events. Help them to see the providential hand of God opening opportunities for them to touch the nations of the earth with His love and the gospel. Find those who are traveling to distant cultures and bring them together to share their experiences. Help them make connections with Christians in those regions where they are traveling and working. Provide cross-cultural training. Ask them to share their experiences with the church. Pray for them as your missionaries.

We are living in one of the most exciting moments in history. The world has changed dramatically in the last fifteen years. For some, this creates confusion and fear. But for the believer who has confidence in the God of history, it is a time of unprecedented opportunity for the gospel. God has not given up on humanity. He is re-shaping the world in the twenty-first century to offer all people everywhere the opportunity to experience His love through Jesus Christ.

In the following chapters we will examine seven new realities God is using to fulfill His vision in the lives of His people. It is my prayer that you will hear another voice whispering into your ear. I pray that God will speak to you about His vision that exceeds anything written here or anything you have previously imagined. "Now to him who is able to do exceeding abundantly beyond all that we ask or think, according to the power that works within us, to Him be the glory in the church and in Christ Jesus to all generations forever and ever." (Ephesians 3:20).

Questions for Reflection and Discussion

1. What theme or pattern are you hearing from God in your personal devotional life?

2. As you listen to other believers, what would they list as your spiritual gifts?

3. Describe the next step God would have you take in your journey with him? What does he want to change in your life? What does he want you to do next?

4. What makes your church unique from other churches?

5. Describe the next step God would have your church take to advance the gospel to your community and the world.

CHAPTER THREE

NEW REALITY #1:
A CONNECTED WORLD

For most of human history people lived with no knowledge of distant continents. Entire civilizations developed and declined thinking that their sphere of the planet was the only sphere that existed. The first global maps did not exist until five hundred years ago. Until the middle of the twentieth century, the continents on that map were remote and inaccessible to the average person. Few ever thought they would visit or live beyond their own borders. Communication with the other side of the planet was delayed and difficult.

The modern missionary movement was launched June 13, 1793 when the Danish ship Kron Princessa Maria sailed out of the harbor at Dover with William Carey on board. Five months would pass before William Carey set foot in Calcutta on November 11. When Carey wrote letters back to England, he would have to wait ten months to receive a written response.

Little improvement was made in communications during the next one hundred years. In December 1880 William Buck Bagby and his wife Anne prepared to fulfill God's vision for them in Brazil. The Foreign Mission Board of the Southern Baptist Convention approved their appointment and decided to appoint them to China. The Bagbys decided the board could appoint them to China if they wished, but they were going to Brazil.[1] They departed Chesapeake Bay aboard the *Yamoden* bound for Brazil the second week of January, 1881. They arrived in Rio de Janeiro on March 2. They were able to telegraph news of their arrival to Richmond, the message relayed via telephone to Anne's parents at Independence,

Texas . But general communication was still almost nonexistent. They received only one letter from the Foreign Mission Board during the first twelve months that they were in Brazil.[2]

The world shrank on May 20, 1927 when Charles Lindbergh's Spirit of St Louis splashed through the mud and narrowly cleared a line of trees at the end of Roosevelt Field near New York City. His wheels would not touch earth again until he reached Paris. Twelve years later Eleanor Roosevelt inaugurated transatlantic commercial aviation with her dedication of the Pan American B-314 *Yankee Clipper* on March 26, 1939. Even so, transatlantic air travel remained a novelty into the mid-twentieth century. Jet service made its debut in the late 1950s and revolutionized international air service by the 1970s. Despite the increasing accessibility of air travel in the mid-twentieth century, missionaries still disappeared for four years to distant lands that most of us never expected to visit. After four years of relative isolation from their land of origin, they returned to tell moving stories of their work in foreign lands in the middle of mysterious cultures.

Today affordable and convenient air service exists to virtually any point on the globe within less than twenty hours. In a single day, anyone can be on the opposite side of the earth. On November 16, 2004, NASA's X-43A aircraft set a new speed record for air travel at 6,500 mph using an experimental engine called the scramjet. Scientists were euphoric over the possibility that commercial air travel could deliver passengers between continents in a matter of minutes rather than hours within the next fifteen years.

These advances in air travel shrunk the world. Today people commute between countries on opposite sides of the globe. With homes in the United States, they work portions of the year in Japan, India, Saudi Arabia or any number of other places. Volunteers can spend their vacations anywhere on earth, spend a week or more engaged in missions and return home in time for work.

Introduction of the PC

The advances in transportation alone could not revolutionize the world in which we live. Something else was needed to truly shrink the world into a global village. Several factors converged in the last decade of the twentieth century to produce our world of instant global communication: Introduction of the PC, the Internet and cell phone wireless services.

I can vaguely remember the introduction of television when I was a small child. It spread rapidly, but for most of my younger years, television was limited to three network broadcasters dependent on antenna reception. For a few brief decades rooftops sprouted TV antennae like bony fingers grasping airwaves from the sky. These were later replaced by cable and satellite with one-hundred channel options. Those born in the mid-1970s will remember the introduction and spread of PCs in much the same way. Those who are younger will have difficulty imagining a world in which computer, internet and cell phones did not exist.

The computer has become to the twenty-first century what the printing press was to the Renaissance and the Reformation. ENIAC debuted in 1942 as the first electronic digital computer. Invented in Bell laboratories, it boasted 18,000 standard vacuum tubes and occupied 1,800 square feet of floor space. Its computing power was far less than a standard lap top today.

The Commodore VIC-20, the Osborne; Kaypro; Commodor 64 and Commodore Amiga; Apple Macintosh; IBM PC; DOS; Enable; Windows98 and ME; 5.25" floppies; 3.5" floppies and modems. If you were born after 1980, most of these names and terms mean nothing to you. If you were born in the 1970s, you may vaguely associate them with childhood video games. But, if you were born before 1970, you will recognize many of them as old but brief friends who helped along the computing journey.

The development, expansion and growth of the PC world have been exponential in my lifetime.

But the PC alone could not revolutionize the world. It was a necessary tool, but it needed a means to connect and transmit information.

The Internet

Prior to the Internet most computers functioned as stand alone units. Some computers were exchanging information on a limited basis, most often through local area networks and occasionally through rather slow modems. It was possible to dial up a particular computer via phone lines and connect, but it was not easy and it was not very efficient.

The military began to develop networking systems as early as 1962 in order to create a means of communication that could withstand a nuclear attack. Email had its early beginnings around 1970 allowing researchers to exchange information between UCLA, UC Santa Barbara, Stanford and the University of Utah. The term "Internet" was used for the first time in 1982. Robert Metcalfe designed the coaxial cable in 1976, an important component that would allow computers to move information extremely fast. But it wasn't until 1992 that the Internet Society was chartered and the World Wide Web released by CERN resulting in the creation of hypertext. The introduction of hypertext revolutionized the Internet resulting in a communications explosion. The annual growth rate of Internet usage in the early 1990s exceeded 300,000% per year. It took less than one decade after the World Wide Web was launched for the Internet to become a household term and an essential means of global communication.

Cell Phone Wireless Services

When innovations are introduced, I am usually one of the early groups adopting the advantages. That was true of cell phones which started to enter our lives in the mid 1980s. They were not the light little gadgets that slip into a pocket or a purse. These were more like luggage: bag phones they called them, because the batteries to drive them were so large and unwieldy that they had to be carried in a bag complete with a shoulder strap. Towers were scarce and dead zones were far more numerous and much larger than the areas where connection could be made and maintained. And they were not cheap.

Today, for some individuals, cell phones are replacing land line phones. In many families, each family member has a cell phone. And cell phones are everywhere. This came home to me when I saw a young man perched on a donkey cart in Cairo, Egypt goading his donkey to a faster pace while he bumped along the street and chatted on the cell phone held to his ear.

My wife and I visited Seoul, Korea in July 2004. When we checked into the Olympic Parktel, I immediately arranged for wireless connection to the internet with my lap top so I could check e-mail. One of the first messages I received was from my eighteen-year old daughter who was working in orphanages in Guatemala. She stopped at an Internet café in Antigua and sent a message which I received the same day. When we returned home, she called us on her cell phone. She was sitting on the roof of a house in San Cristobal watching the sun set behind a volcano. A few weeks later, I was visiting Josue Valerio, the Director of Missions for El Paso Baptist Association. While we were having lunch his cell phone rang. It was his daughter calling from Spain. While working on this manuscript, I set up my wireless lap top on the patio at our house in Texas and within minutes transmitted and received messages with people in Argentina, India and Switzerland.

In little more than one decade, the world has been transformed. We are now instantly connected 24/7 with virtually any place on the earth and able to travel to that place in less than twenty-four hours, if we wish.

This instant connection for communications is revolutionizing the world of missions. Missions is no longer distant. It is close up. We are connected constantly and instantly with people around the world.

When I was serving as executive director for Minnesota-Wisconsin Baptist Convention, we lived in Rochester, Minnesota, the home of Mayo Clinic. We became close friends with many physicians at Mayo. One of those was Jim. Jim was completing his residency at Mayo and we had been praying about where he would establish his practice. They felt God was leading them to Washington State.

One night Jim came to my house, obviously excited. We sat on our deck overlooking Rochester and the lights of Mayo Clinic glowing in the distance. I listened to his story. He had been corresponding via email with David Sorley, one of our Southern Baptist medical missionaries in Nairobi, Kenya. David and his wife Darlene were operating a clinic primarily treating AIDS patients. He had learned that David and Darlene had to return to the United States for some emergency personal issues in their family. With their departure the clinic would close. Jim had prayed about it and become convinced God wanted him to delay his practice for one year, put his student loans on hold and let them accrue interest while he took David Sorley's place in Nairobi.

Within a matter of weeks Jim Keene was in Kenya taking David Sorley's place. Within two weeks after Jim arrived, the United States Embassy in Nairobi was bombed. Jim was there to minister to the victims. The Internet made it possible for Jim Keene and David Sorley to form a direct connection for missions.

On December 26, 2004, the earth was literally shaken on its axis by the earthquake that generated a devastating tsunami in the Indian Ocean. Hundreds of thousands were killed in Thailand, India, Sri Lanka, Indonesia and the many islands of that region. When Justice Anderson, a retired missionary, awoke the next morning he found a voice mail message on his phone from his daughter in Thailand. She called from her cell phone and told him he would hear of massive death and destruction in Southeast Asia when he awoke, but that she and her family were safe. Others were not so fortunate to receive timely and comforting news from loved ones.

Immediately, via internet and phone, volunteers and relief agencies began to respond. Within days, WorldconneX redesigned its home page on the Internet so that those with resources and volunteers could connect with various Christian organizations working in Southeast Asia. People and churches are making instant connections around the world and bypassing the structures and procedures of the past. God is re-wiring the world for missions.

---

[1] Daniel B. Lancaster, *The Bagby's of Brazil*, Eakin Press, A Division of Sunbelt Media, Inc., P. O. Box 90159, Austin, Texas 78709. 1999. p. 24.

[2] *Ibid.* p. 38.

Questions for Reflection and Discussion

1. List some examples of 24/7 global communications in your own experience.

2. Have you traveled internationally in the last year? If so, where did you travel and what did you discover? How did your view of the world change? If not, whom do you know who travels internationally?

3. How have the Internet, email and cell phones changed the way you communicate? How have they changed the network of people with whom you communicate?

4. How have the Internet, email and cell phones changed business? How have they changed education?

5. How does 24/7 global communications change the way we do missions?

CHAPTER FOUR

NEW REALITY #2:
GLOBAL BUSINESS

Until fairly recently, businesses were limited to nations. Most corporations operated within national boundaries with little economic overlap on the international scene. The "connected world" we discussed in the previous chapter has changed that. Global communications opened the door for global commerce. Most corporations of any size are now trans-national. They operate in many countries around the world. The old national boundaries of economy and business are vanishing.

Starbucks Coffee is a prime example. The first Starbucks opened in 1971 in Seattle, but Starbucks did not offer public stock options until 1993. The first Starbucks in Japan opened in 1996. As of 2003, there were 503 Starbucks locations in Japan and 157 in China with forty-four stores in Beijing alone. At the close of 2004 Starbucks had 2,437 locations outside the United States in thirty-three countries.

Christians Doing Missions Through Their Jobs

Just imagine. Someone who works at Starbucks in Dallas, Texas could just as well work at Starbucks in Europe or Asia. Starbucks executives and managers are connected with locations in thirty-three countries and many of them travel there for business. Christians in business have opportunities to share their faith and assist in missions in countries where missionaries cannot go. Not only are they able to go to these "closed" countries, they are paid to go there. They don't have to raise funds to be a missionary.

Early in 2004 I met Jesse. Jesse was a recent graduate of Texas A&M with a Mechanical Engineering degree. He had recently taken a job in Houston in the oil and gas industry. But God was working in Jesse's life and he felt strongly that God was calling him to missions. I agreed to meet him in Houston along with my colleague at WorldconneX, Carol Childress. We met at the Edge conference, an event designed by Global Spectrum to connect profession, passion and God's purposes.

Jesse assumed that the only option open to him was to quit his job, return to seminary for three years and hope he might be appointed as a missionary by a mission board or agency. We affirmed that this might be God's will for him. Only he could determine whether God wanted him to go to seminary and apply as a "professional" missionary. But we suggested another way. "Why throw away your engineering degree? Why not consider that God has something to do with your prior education and professional skill? What if you were to find employment as an engineer in the oil and gas industry in another country where you could be a witness and assist in church planting?" If he were to do this, he could establish credibility where he worked side by side with nationals, he would have opportunity to share his faith and, at the same time, he could encourage and assist other believers in the area. He would need no one to support him financially and he could follow God's call much more quickly. He would need a church to "send" him in order to form a base of prayer support and encouragement. We encouraged Jesse to involve himself in a cross-cultural ministry in one of the many ethnic churches in Houston so he could seek out the people for whom God would give him a passion. We also encouraged him to take advantage of training opportunities like the Perspectives course that helps people discover what God is doing around the world and consider their part in God's purposes. Perspectives is sponsored by the U.S. Center for World Mission, an organization founded by Ralph Winter, and is offered in many churches.

At the same conference we met John, a fifty-year-old oil and gas executive who spent nine years working in the industry in Indonesia. A passionate believer, John had started his own petroleum company with the express purpose of hiring Christians so he could place them in countries where missionaries could not go.

David and Mary Carpenter felt strongly the call from God to missions. David had a successful law practice and owned his own firm. Not having any other concept of how to respond to God's call, David sold his law practice and they enrolled in seminary so they could be appointed by a mission board. David refers to this jokingly as an effort to "get the lawyer taken out of him" so he could do missions. They were sent to Albania. When they arrived they soon discovered that one of the great needs in Albania was for someone to teach in the law school. Suddenly it came into focus for them. His profession, which he thought he must give up to be a missionary, was his open door for ministry.

Mary is now the Minister of Missions at First Baptist Church, Woodway in Waco, Texas. The church has several families serving in Turkey and others preparing to go to Morocco. Their passion is to equip the laity to carry their professions to the ends of the earth.

Another missionary was appointed to carry the gospel to one of the most unreached corners of the earth, a nation dominated by Islam. When he arrived at his destination following a long and arduous journey, he discovered a Baptist deacon from Houston, Texas who was already there working for Shell Oil.

Finding employment in order to carry out missionary work is nothing new. The Apostle Paul intentionally sought employment in order to follow God's call to various places where he served. A brilliant theologian, mentored under Gamaliel in Jerusalem, Paul took time to learn the tent making trade in order to support himself. When he came to Corinth, he found employment with Priscilla and Aquilla, doubtless teaching this young couple about

Christ while he worked with them in the manufacture and repair of tents. (Acts 18:2-3). Paul was willing to accept financial assistance when it was available in order to carry the gospel to new regions. But he never let the lack of financial support stop him from going.

The global economy of the twenty-first century is re-creating a similar context in which the first century disciples carried the gospel to the ends of their known world. While the Roman Empire was crumbling from within due to moral decadence, the *Pax Romana* had created a global context for commerce in which people could move about freely and find employment. Today, for the first time since the first centuries, people with marketable skills can go to the ends of the earth with the gospel.

Christians Creating Businesses For Missions

Christian businesspeople have sometimes felt like second class citizens in our churches. We give them the impression that truly spiritual work is done at church or in church-sponsored programs, while business is non-spiritual, even crass. As a result, some of the most creatively entrepreneurial members of the churches keep a low profile at church. This needs to be corrected. The church in the twenty-first century needs to recognize that these successful business people can create the greatest opportunities for missions the world has seen.

We should pause to recognize that the Bible never separated successful business from the mission of God. Abraham was a successful businessman who grew wealthy in his later years. Likewise Jacob successfully multiplied his father-in-law's herds before building his own estate. By the time Jacob left Haran, he was "exceedingly prosperous, and had large flocks and female and male servants and camels and donkeys." (Genesis 30:43). Joseph, sold into slavery, emerged as the prime minister of Egypt. Moses spent forty years as a herdsman before God sent him to deliver Israel. David was a shepherd, a soldier and a king. Isaiah was a counselor of kings and Amos was a herdsman. In the New Testament, Peter was a successful fisherman. Luke was a physician. Lydia was a successful business woman in purple fabrics. She became the first convert in Europe and formed the beginning of the church at Philippi.

In recent years, Christian missionaries attempted to enter closed countries posing as legitimate businesses while, in fact, having no business expertise or interest. This has proven to be unfortunate in most cases and counterproductive to the gospel. Honesty and integrity cannot be discarded, even when the ends seem to justify the means by giving Christians a foothold in a hostile country. Addressing this issue, Steve Rundle and Tom Steffen, co-authors of *Great Commission Companies*, note that "many of these same countries are quite willing to tolerate legitimate Christian-managed businesses. We have found that the most effective Great Commission Companies are in fact quite open about their faith and have a reputation for evangelistic work. ... While these countries are aggressively trying to attract entrepreneurship and capital from abroad, they have little tolerance for people who make no obvious contribution."[1] Rundle and Steffen define a Great Commission Company as "a socially responsible, income producing business managed by kingdom professionals and created for the specific purpose of glorifying God and promoting the growth and multiplication of local churches in the least evangelized and least-developed parts of the world."[2]

Michael R. Baer is executive director of International Micro Enterprises Development, Inc. He states, "We are entering the 'kingdom company' era in world missions, especially in regards to unreached peoples in restricted-access countries. ... 'kingdom business' ... is not a 'shell business' but rather a for profit operation that ministers *through its operation* rather than in spare time *from it*."[3]

Writing for Christianity Today, John Cragin states, "The concept of *business missions*, once commonly thought to be an oxymoron, is growing into its own. Businesspeople around the world are eager to

39

add eternal significance to their temporal success. Mission agencies and evangelical churches are beginning to take their approach seriously. Business and trade opens doors to relationships that may be closed to traditional missionaries. Moreover, the authentic witness of lay professionals often has more credibility for host-country contacts in the marketplace than that of traditional missionaries." He goes on to say, "I have seen 27 families resign their high-paying jobs, sell their homes, acquire cross-cultural and language training, get inoculated against typhoid, typhus, and other diseases, and fly 8,000 miles to start a Great Commission Company. They created opportunities to share the gospel with thousands and encouraged and trained local believers. And they financed or spun off a dozen other equally effective ventures."[4]

Patrick Lai tells of his experience in starting businesses in a predominantly Muslim country in order to spread the gospel. He recalls how he started his journey viewing "tent-making" as less than whole-hearted ministry, and reflects on the discouragement he received from fellow Christians when he proposed going into business rather than serving as a traditional missionary. But he persevered. He formed a partnership with a close friend and they sat down to develop their vision and values. " Before we opened our first business," he says, "we wrote down two criteria. First, every business needed to be profitable within eighteen months. Second, every business needed to create witnessing opportunities. If a business failed at either point, we would shut it down."[5] They started an English school, a kindergarten, a boat transport company, a taxi service, a thrift store and a grocery store. In every case they invested less than $10,000 and hired only people in the country who were unemployed. They avoided hiring any expatriate employees. Three of the businesses failed. Two of these failed economically. The third succeeded financially but did not provide a means of spreading the gospel. The other three met both their criteria. They became successful businesses and produced a thriving church in the city. Patrick was eventually deported by the government because of the overt evangelistic impact of the businesses. But the indigenous believers continued to grow the churches and the businesses after he left.

Pura-Vida Coffee was created in 1998 by John Sage and Chris Dearnley. Committed followers of Jesus Christ, John and Chris started Pura Vida Coffee in order to build a business that would impact coffee producing countries with the gospel while creating a funding source for Christian organizations that are working in these countries. Countries in which they currently work include Costa Rica, Ethiopia and Indonesia. Pura Vida states its mission as follows: "We believe in a different approach to business. One driven by good rather than greed. One that sees capitalism as an agent for compassion and faith as an engine for action. Pura Vida is 100% charitably owned and all of our resources go to help at-risk children and families in coffee-growing countries build more hopeful futures. The work of Pura Vida is rooted in personal faith and a desire to empower the poor in coffee-growing regions of the world. We welcome all people to serve with us in partnership."[6] They list five core values:

- We are motivated by personal faith and invite all people to join with us in partnership
- We embrace Christ's call to serve the poor and reduce inequity
- We believe capitalism can be driven by a desire to create good rather than greed
- We believe that consumers and business leaders can join together to promote a new type of capitalism; this has the power to change the way we think about business
- We believe in an empowering, long-term and sustainable approach to community development[7]

I first met Bob in December of 2004. Bob is eighty years old. Ten years ago, while working as the President of a wireless telephone company, he was invited by the government of Guinea to help privatize the phone system. He moved to Guinea and lived there for a year and a half. In the process he earned the trust of the government leaders and became friends with the president and the army chief of staff. Although Guinea is 85% Muslim, they have grown to trust this elderly Christian who has started a church for refugees and a school that enrolls approximately 250 students. He has identified hundreds of villages with an open door to the gospel. Most of these have a mosque but have never heard the gospel.

Bob later formed another company, Frontier Land Development and leased more than 250,000 acres of land from the government of Guinea. Bob is currently seeking Christian farmers who will sublease the land, establish farms, employ the people of Guinea and create schools on their farms where they can teach and train their employees. The project will provide jobs to the large number of unemployed in Guinea, will improve the quality of life and the economy while providing Christians the opportunity to share their faith and disciple new believers.

In June of 2004 I accompanied several pastors on a visit to a Muslim nation as guests of the government We met with a number of government officials and religious leaders, including the Imam. I was most impressed with our visits with the governors. In each visit we asked them to tell us their top priority and the greatest needs for their people. They emphasized the need for peace. The quality of life for their people, they explained, was stymied until peace could be achieved in that region of the world. Second to this was their interest in business. They were not only open to businesses from the United States and the West, they welcomed and encouraged it. They needed employment for their young people who were graduating from their universities with professional skills and few opportunities for work. Many places in the world offer an open door to those who have the entrepreneurial knowledge and skills to create successful businesses.

This may well be the most revolutionary missions development in the twenty-first century. Professional, fully funded missionaries are still needed and will still be sent by existing denominational and para-church missions boards and agencies. They might even add to their numbers. But the missions impact of entrepreneurial Christians who capitalize on the global economy and the new realities could be exponential by comparison.

---

[1] Steve Rundle and Tom Steffen, *Great Commission Companies*, InterVarsity Press, P.O. box 1400, Downers Grove, IL 60515. p. 23

[2] Ibid. p. 41.

[3] Tetsunao Yamamori and Kenneth A. Eldred, editors, *On Kingdom Business, Transforming Missions Through Entrepreneurial Strategies*. Crossway Books, A Division of Good News Publishers, 1300 Crescent Street, Wheaton, IL 60187. p.195.

[4] http://www.christianitytoday.com/ct/2004/004/38.103.html

[5]. Tetsunao Yamamori and Kenneth A. Eldred, *op cit.* p.57.

[6] http://www.puravidacoffee.com/work/work_body.asp

[7] http://www.puravidacoffee.com/work/work_mission.asp

Questions for Reflection and Discussion

1. What are the international needs and opportunities in your profession?

2. How does your profession bring you in contact with other nationalities?

3. Who are the business people in your church that travel and work internationally? Where do they work? What possibilities does this create for missions involvement?

CHAPTER FIVE

NEW REALITY #3:
POPULATION MIGRATION

God is moving the populations of the earth and creating a cosmopolitan climate for missions that has not existed since the Mediterranean world of the first century. He is doing this first through the remarkable growth of cities. He is doing it secondly through the dispersion of ethnic groups among many nations.

Migration to the Cities

We are witnessing the greatest population migration in human history, the movement of massive numbers of people to the cities. In 1800 only 3% of the world's population lived in cities. By 1900 this had grown to 14%. As of 2000 almost one-half (47%) of the world's population lived in cities.[1] This is not just a regional phenomenon confined to a quadrant, sphere or continent. It is global. This fact alone will change the context for missions in the twenty-first century and set it apart from any previous time in human history. In the words of urban missiologist, Ray Bakke, "God is re-wiring the world."

The ten largest cities in the world are located in Japan (Tokyo), the United States (New York and Los Angeles), Mexico (Mexico City), India (Bombay and Calcutta), China (Shanghai), Brazil (Sao Paulo), Nigeria (Lagos) and Argentina (Buenos Aires).[2] World-wide, 411 cities now exceed 1 million in population.[3] China alone has forty cities with more than one million people.

The Bible and Cities

God is not caught off guard by this remarkable movement to the cities. In fact, God is in charge of what is occurring. It is part of his divine and ultimate plan by which the nations of the earth will turn to Him. While the Bible is chiefly an agrarian book filled with pastoral metaphors, it is also a book rooted in the cities.

Abraham originates from Sumeria, the center of ancient civilization where writing was first devised and where cities first flourished. Quite specifically, he is identified as coming from Ur of the Chaldees, the largest Sumerian city that included libraries, schools and numerous temples. Abraham's response to leave the land of his fathers is followed by four hundred years in which his offspring multiply as an oppressed ethnic minority in Egypt. While their spiritual understanding was forged in the wilderness, their very existence was fashioned in the ghettos of Egypt as part of the slave labor that built the ancient pyramids for their aristocratic overlords. The great deliverer, Moses, grew to maturity in the urban center of Egypt, educated in the sciences and languages of Egypt as the adopted son of the Pharaoh.

Their movement into the promised land reached its zenith with the establishment of the City of David. And, generations later, the prophet issued his proclamation in terms of the city saying: " Turn, O backsliding children, saith the LORD; for I am married unto you: and I will take you one of a city, and two of a family, and I will bring you to Zion." (Jeremiah 3:14). When Jesus entered the final phase of his public ministry, Luke wrote: "As he approached Jerusalem and saw the city, he wept over it." (Luke 19:41).

Paul's strategy to reach the first century world focused on reaching the cities: Philippi, Corinth, Thessalonica, Ephesus and Rome. Many of the New Testament books derive their names from the cities that received Paul's letters.

The Book of Revelation proclaims our ultimate eternal dwelling with God in terms of the city, saying: "I saw the Holy City, the new Jerusalem, coming down out of heaven from God, prepared as a bride beautifully dressed for her husband." (Revelation 21:2).

Clearly the cities have always played an important role in God's plan to redeem mankind. The God of history has, at the very least, allowed the development of these teeming urban centers that dominate our landscape, and, according to the witness of Scripture, He weeps over them with a desire that all who inhabit them should be redeemed through His Son.

Re-shuffling the ancient traditions

The movement to the cities world-wide is creating greater openness to the gospel. Family traditions and religions that proved all but impenetrable in the rural context break down with the movement to the cities. Philip Jenkins recognizes this as an important element in the rapid growth of Christianity in the southern hemisphere. "In Latin America especially, the move to the cities over the past half century has liberated ordinary people from traditional religious structures. ... In Africa too, the independent churches find their firmest support in the swollen cities, among migrants and the dispossessed."[4]

The Urban Mosaic

This movement to the cities is not simply a re-location of existing cultures within regions and nations. The rise of cities is creating multi-cultural, multi-lingual and multi-ethnic societies unique to the world's history. It is entirely possible to live in a city and remain blind to this multi-cultural mosaic. In America, we tend to live in virtual mono-cultural suburbs and neighborhoods. Most of the people who live near us look like us, talk like us and live like us. We commute to work on freeways in automotive isolation, winding above, around and past the enclaves of other cultures and ethnicities to reach our offices and businesses where we spend the day working with people who have a similar education and experience to our own.

But, if we exit the freeways and wander down side streets in the city, we discover a wide diversity in culture and language. Houston, Texas is home to more than one hundred different language groups. Asians are the fastest growing ethnic group in Houston, growing by 76% between 1990 and 2000 and representing 6% of the population.[5] The Hispanic population jumped from 27.1% in 1990 to 37.4% in 2000. Anglos will soon be a minority.

Chicago is the second largest Polish city in the world. Nearly 139,000 of them are foreign born. And of these, 69,000 arrived after 1990.[6] The ethnic diversity of Chicago is clearly represented in its grocery stores: African, Caribbean, Thai, Vietnamese, Indian, Middle Eastern, Russian, Korean, Greek and Mexican, to list a few.

When I think of Brazil, I think of beautiful dark skinned people full of laughter and music who speak Portuguese. I was a bit stunned when I learned that one million of the sixteen million people who live in Sao Paulo are Japanese making it the largest Japanese community outside of Japan. In fact, Sao Paulo is one of the most ethnically diverse cities in the world with more than seventy nationalities including large concentrations of Arabs, Eastern Europeans and Italians.

Going to the Ends of the Earth Next Door

The *diaspora* was a significant element in the successes of the first century church. Early believers recognized the opportunities created by the dispersion of Jews and other peoples throughout the Roman Empire. James specifically addressed his letter to the "twelve tribes who are *dispersed* abroad." (James 1:1). Peter addressed his first letter to those who are "scattered throughout Pontus, Galatia, Cappadocia, Asia and Bythinia." (1 Peter 1:1). Paul recognized the advantage of this dispersion and consistently sought enclaves of Jews in the cities where he went in order to establish a core group of believers. We need to recognize that God is dispersing people groups throughout the world in cities where they can more readily hear the gospel and become disciples of Jesus Christ.

I was pastor of Franklin Baptist Church in Franklin, Texas in the early 1970s. The first waves of Vietnamese refugees began to arrive following the war in Vietnam. We picked them up with our church bus and brought them to our church where they attended our services. They patiently listened to our English and sat through our Western worship. What they learned or absorbed, I don't know.

We began to learn how to work across cultural differences. By the early eighties I was serving on the staff of the Baptist General Convention of Texas with a team of colleagues intent on reaching our increasingly diverse state. Sok Deoung from Cambodia, Santi Rapanyanchi from Thailand, Yutaka Takarada from Japan, Bernie Moraga from Chile and others helped me learn the importance of finding culturally relevant methods to develop indigenous leaders who could reach the people God was bringing to the United States.

Anglo churches began sponsoring ethnic congregations that could worship in their native language, compose and sing Christian songs that reflected their culture and fellowship around tables sharing their traditional foods. They began to take root and grow. But starting a church that could reach a specific ethnic group was not the end. These churches, in many cases, created connections for the gospel back to their native lands.

When I lived in Minnesota, I learned that the largest concentration of Hmong in the United States had chosen to live in the upper mid-west. Natives of Laos, the Hmong were America's closest allies during the Vietnamese conflict. Following the fall of South

Vietnam, thousands of Hmong emigrated to the U. S. to escape political persecution by the Communists. Animists by heritage, many of the Hmong responded to the gospel. Nhia Ye Her and Ton Zong Vang gave excellent leadership to the emerging Hmong Baptist Fellowship with fifteen Hmong churches in Minnesota and Wisconsin, some averaging as many as 200 in attendance. In 1998 the Hmong Baptist churches formed a partnership with Minnesota-Wisconsin Baptists and began sending volunteer teams to reach their homeland in Laos.

Frank Dang is one of our colleagues at WorldconneX. Frank was born in Vietnam in 1971. His father served as a medic for the South Vietnamese and U.S. forces. When Vietnam fell, his father was imprisoned for two years and the family banished to poverty with no privileges for education or hope for advancement. His father escaped as one of the boat people in 1979 and nearly drowned at sea. He and his companions were rescued by a ship carrying Christians who cared for them and witnessed to them in the refugee camps. His father became a believer and relocated to New Orleans. Frank was left to grow up in poverty as a Buddhist in Vietnam. It took ten years for his father to save enough money to bring his family to the United States.

At age eighteen, Frank joined his father in New Orleans and, for the first time heard the name of Jesus. He discovered the answer to his quest for God and found the emptiness in his life filled by faith in Jesus Christ. After two years of study in which he learned English and passed his high school GRE, Frank received a full scholarship to Tulane University. Four years later he received a degree *summa cum laude* in mathematics. He began his PhD studies in mathematics at Tulane. But a visit back to Vietnam with his father changed the course of his life.

When he and his father visited his native land, he was overcome with a passion to reach his people with the gospel. He longed to see the children, who were growing up in the same conditions he experienced, given the opportunity to hear about Jesus Christ and to follow Him in faith. He soon left Tulane and enrolled in seminary. Subsequent visits to Afghanistan and Egypt expanded his vision for a world in need of Christ. He is now rallying Vietnamese and Korean churches to send medical teams to the Muslim world.

Morocco is one of the most closed countries to the gospel. Occupying the northwest corner of Africa and guarding the entrance to the Mediterranean Sea, Morocco is 99.85% muslim. Sunni Islam is the state religion. It is illegal to proselytize a Moroccon muslim to the Christian faith. The few Christians who are present are tolerated as long as they confine their work to expatriate populations. Likely no more than 5% of the population have heard the gospel.

But large numbers of Moroccans have moved to Europe to find employment. An estimated 1.5 million live in France, 240,000 in the Netherlands, 150,000 in Belgium, 113,000 in Spain and 100,000 in Germany. [7] While it is extremely difficult and dangerous to witness to Moroccans in Morocco, in these lands the gospel can be shared openly. Once reached, Moroccan Christians can become the means for the gospel to penetrate their own family and community relationships. I am not implying that it is easy to reach native Moroccans when they are abroad, but we should recognize the opportunities to reach these and other people groups whom God is dispersing around the world.

According to the 2000 census, 2.43 million Chinese live in the United States. The number of Chinese-Americans increased by 800,000 during the decade of the nineties. The large increase was fueled primarily by an influx of professionals and technology workers as well as relatives of families already living in the United States. Chinese is replacing French in Canada as the second most spoken language in homes outside Quebec.

Khalil Jaloub serves as the Missions Pastor for the Hunters Glen Baptist Church in Plano, Texas. Khalil was born in Baghdad and grew up a Muslim. As a young man he left Iraq for studies in England and the United States. In an effort to find inner peace, purpose and meaning for his life, he devoted himself more fully to Islam but found few answers. Allah, he says, did not answer his deepest needs. So, living in Oklahoma, he decided to try other religions starting with Christianity. He walked across the street to visit the services of a Baptist church. The warm embrace by the greeter took him by surprise, and the message about a God who loves us was shocking. Not long after, he made a profession of faith. While the church rallied around him in celebration of his faith commitment, no one took time to teach him or disciple him. Fortunately he married a devout Christian woman who was able to lead him to a full understanding of what it means to be a follower of Jesus Christ trusting in His grace alone for salvation. How many Khalil's are there near the place where each of us live and worship? How many times do we pass them over not taking note of their need to know Jesus Christ?

The Ethnic America Network was started in 1999 by a group of believers who were burdened about reaching across the many cultures that now reside in the United States while continuing to reach around the world. Their vision is "to see a growing number of churches intentionally crossing cultures to pray and care for others, while sharing the love of Jesus Christ, both locally and around the world." The network involves more than sixty evangelical denominations and agencies. Each year the Ethnic America Network hosts an Ethnic Worker's Summit so that those who are involved in cross-cultural missions can learn from one another.[8] In the twenty-first century, we can literally go to the ends of the earth next door.

Urbanization and the Transformation Challenge

We need to pause for a moment and consider the importance of reaching people in our cities with the gospel of Jesus Christ. The issue is really about life and death. Certainly that is true in terms of our eternal relationship with God in Heaven. Jesus alone is the way, the truth and the life. No one comes to the Father but by Him. It is also true in terms of the quality of life on earth. Faith in Jesus Christ creates communities where each human life is respected, where people practice honesty, truth, generosity and compassion. Faith in Christ creates the moral foundations upon which life on earth can be lived in peace and harmony.

Racial Tension and the Polarization of "haves" and "have-nots."

The United States is becoming increasingly multi-ethnic and racially segregated. The fires of racial hatred and suspicion smolder beneath the surface, no less threatening today than they were in the 1960s. In Minneapolis, one of the least heterogeneous cities in America, distinct business districts have sprung up that are easily identified as Hispanic, Somali, Hmong, Vietnamese and Ethiopian. Immigration to America has shifted from the Anglo and Western European movements of the nineteenth and early twentieth century to immigration from Asia, Africa and Latin America. Most of these immigrants settle first in the inner cities. Some with educational backgrounds move through quickly finding profes- sional employment and adequate income. Others become trapped and desperate.

The fastest growing ethnic group in America today is Hispanic, far outstripping the black population with high birth rates and its endless immigration streams from Mexico, Central and South America, some legal, some not. Coupled with this is the fact that both the Hispanic and Black communities, as a whole, are lagging behind the technological revolution and falling into deeper trenches of economic despair.

In other nations, like Brazil, wealth and opportunity remain in the city center while communities mired in poverty form on the outskirts. Moving from the rainforests, the poorest Brazilians have relocated to form *favelas* on the edges of Manaus hoping to secure opportunity for jobs and a meager income. One tourist site posted this warning for visitors: "Stay away from the *favelas* (slums) in Manaus. These are dung infested, dirty, and impovished areas. Crime is huge and common in these areas. The poorest *favelas* look like garbage dumps, the homes are on stilts to get above the flooding and to get away from all the trash and decay in the ground. Stay away from these areas."

Perhaps nowhere in the world is the class structure more clearly defined and impenetrable than in India. The Hindu caste system of India isolates the poorest of the poor, the Dhalits, who are often deprived of the very basic needs for living, including drinking water, food and shelter. Hinduism offers no possibility of improvement to these religious and social outcasts. Dhalits comprise 15% of India's population. Bangalore is a city of six million recognized as the "silicon valley" of India. In Bangalore the groups of Dhalits are relegated to cleaning out toilet pits with their bare hands.

Moral Decay: Lessons from Mexico City, Manaus and Moscow

The greatest threat and the greatest challenge to the future of our cities and our nation is not economic. It is moral. Any problem can be solved and overcome by a people who are bound together by moral principles of honesty, generosity, truth and compassion. There is no hope for a people whose core is eaten away by deceit, jealousy, greed and corruption.

In the early 1800s Alexis de Tocqueville toured the United States in search of the secret that made democracy work. His conclusion was simple. It was the moral values of the people which sprang from their religious faith. Without that, he concluded, the democratic experiment was doomed to fail.

Robert Kaplan, the heralded foreign correspondent for Atlantic Monthly, made a similar trek across America in the mid 1990s and wrote his conclusions in his book, *An Empire Wilderness, Travels Into America's Future*. His findings stand in stark contrast to de Tocqueville's two centuries earlier. He wrote of his visit to California: "In superaffluent Orange County (where household wealth is much higher than the national average and poverty far below) we have clearly moved to a stage of economic development that encourages an obsession with oneself. ... Despite Orange County's wealth, 'there is almost no philanthropy here.'"[9]

Extending his journey through the U.S. and Mexico, Kaplan concluded, "The differences between Mexico and the United States are basic: we, despite our inequalities, are a civil society in which citizens feel reasonably secure under a rule of law; Mexico is not. ... The police of Mexico are not merely corrupt, they *are* criminals."[10] Notably the election of Vicente Fox was largely based on his promise to end corruption in Mexico.

Kaplan, himself a professed non-believer, made an interesting observation when he passed a church building in his trek through Mexico. He says, "We came to a lovely Mexican church. Its whitewashed walls glittering in the sun, its bell tower and courtyard reminded me of the grace and purity of religious buildings in Spain and North Africa. The church conjured up tradition, sensuality, nostalgia. If only this church were more relevant to the social forces roiling the southern half of Tucson."[11]

When I visited Russia, I found myself deeply moved by the hopelessness written on the faces of the people as they moved in endless lines through the tunnels of the metro system of Moscow.

I found my heart deeply stirred by the stories of pastors whose fathers had been imprisoned under communism for smuggling Bibles to fellow believers. I was stirred by Aleksandr Solzhenitsyn in his *Gulag Archipelago* as he detailed the atrocities of the Gulags in the region of Siberia where our Minnesota-Wisconsin team planted a church in the city of Irkutsk. I shuddered as I learned of the crime and corruption that rules post-communist Russia. I was warned by the missionaries not to look directly into the eyes of the police because they were known to intimidate tourists in order to extort bribes.

I asked myself, "Why is it that democracy in these countries does not work? Why is it that Brazil, Russia, Mexico and other countries which now boast a democratic society are controlled by corruption, crime and exploitation?" The answer became quite clear: democracy cannot work without a moral foundation. In Russia, where communism ruled with an atheistic iron fist for seventy-five years, democracy has been ostensibly instituted, but there is no spiritual or moral foundation to sustain it.

A few years ago I visited the Kilauea Volcano on the Big Island of Hawaii. In 1982 this volcano erupted with sheets of molten rock catapulted over 100 feet in the air. An entire village was wiped out. I stood on the lava fields and looked over the scorched and scarred landscape, barren of life, where repeatedly the molten lava has burst through the surface. I stood at the fire pit, the Hilamaumau crater, where I smelled the steam and sulfur that continue to sift through cracks in the rocky surface of the volcano. I watched as visitors came from around the world and offered rice to the fire god they worshipped at this barren and deadly place.

It was a visual picture of our nation and the world as we enter the twenty-first century. Many are somehow aware that the deadly force is still beneath the surface, thankful it is temporarily contained. Many are offering sacrifices to false gods.

Although we have sealed off the molten lava of crime beneath the rocky surface of police protection and an inflated penal system, the unrest is still there. The racial prejudice that shook our nation in the sixties is still present. The moral foundations upon which our democracy has stood for two hundred years are cracked and on the verge of crumbling. We have witnessed the sulfur and steam rising from fissures in the surface, indicating the enormous unrest below.

We saw it in Los Angeles in March 1991 when thousands took to the streets looting and burning the city after the Rodney King verdict. Some of us can still see the ominous columns of smoke rising over East LA, the view from helicopter cameras of people rioting and looting in the streets and the unforgettable sight of Reginald Denny, a white truck driver who stopped for a red light in the wrong place at the wrong time, dragged from his tractor trailer rig and beaten in the street with bricks.

We now live in a post 9-11 world. The world did not change on September 11, 2001 when terrorists flew their hijacked airliners into the twin towers of New York and the Pentagon in Washington, D. C. What changed was our understanding. Our pre 9-11 perspective assumed we were disconnected from the cultural clashes taking place on the opposite side of the planet. Before 9-11, America felt securely protected by the Atlantic and Pacific oceans that separate us from foreign nations. That protective barrier had already disappeared, although we did not realize it until the catastrophic collapse of the towers. We now know that the destinies of our cities are intertwined and we cannot go back to the world as it was. Cultures and ethnicities no longer live in isolation.

When we talk about our multi-cultural and growing cities, we are talking about the future of our world, the world our children will inherit and the eternal destiny of millions on the earth. How shall we address these issues?

The body of Christ must marshal all of its resources to address the social, moral and spiritual challenges of the twenty-first century. Luis Bush, who gave leadership to AD 2000, followed up that effort by conducting listening sessions with Christians on every continent of the world. The consensus was clear. The key word is "transformation." The body of Christ must focus on transformation. Believers engaged in missions are hearing the voice of the Holy Spirit clearly. Followers of Jesus Christ are devoting themselves to nation building and community transformation that includes the holistic needs Jesus addressed when He walked among us. We must address spiritual and moral issues that include human rights, poverty, health, orphan and child care, healthy families and respect for all men and women. God is speaking to His body in these days the same word that Jesus chose at the outset of his earthly ministry: "The Spirit of the Lord is upon me because He has anointed me to preach the gospel to the poor; he has sent me to heal the broken hearted, to preach deliverance to the captives, and recovering of sight to the blind, to set at liberty them that are bruised, to preach the acceptable year of the Lord." (Luke 4:18).

---

[1] United Nations, *World Urbanization Prospects, The 1999 Revision.* (http://www.prb.org/Content/NavigationMenu/PRB/Educators/Human_Population/Urbanization2/Patterns_of_World_Urbanization1.htm)

[2] World Almanac and Book of Facts, U. S. Census, United Nations, (http://www.mongabay.com/igapo/cities.htm)

[3] United Nations, *World Urbanization Prospects, The 1999 Revision. Ibid.*

[4] Philip Jenkins, *The Next Christendom, the Coming of Global Christianity*, Oxford University Press, 198 Madison Avenue, NY, NY 10016. p. 73.

[5] Texas A&M University, Real Estate Center. (http://www.mongabay.com/igapo/cities.htm)

[6] Polish News, 6205 N. Milwaukee, Avenue, Unit 1-F, Chicago, IL 60646.

[7] Patrick Johnstone and Jason Mandruk, *Operation World*, Paternoster Publishing PO Box 1047, Waynesboro GA 30830-2047, 2001. p. 455-457

[8] http://www.ethnic-america.net/

[9] Robert D. Kaplan, *An Empire Wilderness, Travels Into America's Future*, Random House, Inc. New York. 1998. p. 97

[10] *Ibid.* p. 111.

[11] *Ibid.* p. 158.

Questions for Reflection and Discussion

1. What ethnic groups are present in your community? How are these reflected in your schools and businesses?

2. How is your church reaching these ethnic groups to make disciples? How are other churches reaching them?

3. What efforts could be made to minister to Muslims, Buddhists and other religious groups in your city?

4. Where are the poorest neighborhoods nearest you? What is being done to transform these communities?

5. How is your church engaged in community transformation ministry in cities outside the United States?

CHAPTER SIX

NEW REALITY # 4:
CHRISTIANITY'S NEW GEOGRAPAHICAL CENTER

Most of my life has been lived in the second half of the twentieth century. In the world in which I grew up we made several basic assumptions about the world. One of these assumptions was the idea that the United States was the center of Christianity with the greatest number of churches and Christians. This assumption is no longer true.

The West, including the United States and Europe, is no longer the center of the Christian faith. The center has shifted to the southern hemisphere. The number of Christians and the number of churches in Latin America, Africa and Asia outnumber the Christians and churches in the United States and Europe. At the same time that the world has undergone technological, economic and social transformation, it has also experienced a profound spiritual shift. It is a bit humbling to suddenly realize that God is using other people and nations to accomplish the Great Commission. For decades we have made the assumption that if the world is to be reached for Christ, it will be up to Christians in America to do it. While our part is still important, God is using many others to accomplish His purposes in the world.

Missions is about God, not about us. And God is at work in the world doing incredible things that have not been seen since the first century. Philip Jenkins, in his book *The Next Christendom, The Coming of Global Christianity*, states, "We are currently living through one of the transforming moments in the history of religion worldwide. ... Over the past century ... the center of gravity in

61

the Christian world has shifted inexorably southward, to Africa, Asia, and Latin America. Already today, the largest Christian communities on the planet are to be found in Africa and Latin America. If we want to visualize a 'typical' contemporary Christian, we should think of a woman living in a village in Nigeria or in a Brazilian *favela*."[1] This, Jenkins says, is more typical of modern Christianity than my experience of the North American church.

Projecting the future of Christianity in the twenty-first century, Jenkins states that, "Christianity should enjoy a worldwide boom in the new century, but the vast majority of believers will be neither white nor European, nor Euro-American. ... By 2050, only about one-fifth of the world's 3 billion Christians will be non-Hispanic whites. Soon, the phrase 'a white Christian" may sound like a curious oxymoron, as mildly surprising as 'a Swedish Buddhist.'"[2]

Jenkins and others testify to the fact that this mushrooming movement of new believers in South America, Africa and Asia is characterized by a conservative belief in the Bible as God's authority for life along with supernatural demonstrations of God's power including visions, dreams and healing. The forms and structures for church and worship are not reproductions of the West, but new, innovative and culturally diverse.

South America

In April, 2004 I was invited to speak about WorldconneX to a meeting of the Union Bautista Latinoamericana (Baptist Union of Latin America, UBLA) in Cali, Colombia. Baptist leaders from across Latin America gathered in Colombia to discuss their common concerns. Significant to the discussion was a total absence of dialogue about how they could attract the help of churches in the United States. Instead, their discussion centered around how they could more effectively reach South America and send their own missionaries to reach the Muslim world.

Daniel Bianchi, missions director for Argentina, was one of the presenters at the meeting. He listed a number of challenges and trends affecting missions in the twenty-first century. He described a world of constant change in which national missionary movements mature and churches become engaged in global missions. When I stood up to explain why we created WorldconneX, I simply said, "For all the reasons Daniel Bianchi just listed."

Colombia is number three of the ten most dangerous countries to visit in the world, according to Robert Pelton in his book, *The World's Most Dangerous Places*, a resource cited by CNN and used by journalists, the CIA and Navy SEALS.[3]   On March 3, 2004, The United States Department of State listed Colombia as one of twenty-six countries that American travelers should avoid. And yet God is moving among the churches and people of Colombia.

David Garrison includes Colombia as one of the nations where God is moving through a Church planting movement. Church planting movements occur when churches rapidly reproduce by starting other church so that the number of believers multiplies. He cites the violence and persecution in Colombia as factors that have led churches to multiply in cell groups rather than constructing buildings. This cell group multiplication is a common pattern in Church planting movements. But the spiritual growth in Colombia is not mere method. Referring to the International Charistmatic Mission that started in 1983, grew to 8,000 members by 1990 and mushroomed to 45,000 members by 1999, he writes, "its leadership resists being identified with methods. Church leaders have infused its members with a passionate sense of God's presence and guidance. The church is characterized by indigenous Colombian leadership at every level, rapidly reproducing cell groups, and core values of prayer, fasting and holiness."[4]

In June of 2004, I met with the leaders of the Guatemala Baptist Convention in Guatemala City. I learned that descendants of the ancient Mayan Indian people, the Kekchi, are turning to Christ. The largest church among Guatemala Baptists is a Kekchi Baptist church with more than 5,000 members. The church operates its own radio station broadcasting Christian programming in the Kekchi language, and sponsors more than twenty missions. The Korean Baptist Fellowship, made up of Korean Baptist churches in the United States have sent their own missionary to work among the Kekchi and regularly send volunteer medical teams to Guatemala. Garrison notes, "During the decades of the 1960s through 1980s, Kekchi evangelicals saw their numbers triple from about 20,000 to more than 60,000."[5]

In Brazil the evangelical churches have been growing at twice the rate of the population. As of 1997, Brazilian churches were sending 1,200 missionaries serving in 71 countries including Europe, Africa, Asia, North America, the Caribbean and the Middle East. Another 500 missionaries work cross-culturally within the country.[6]

Africa

According to the Christian History Institute, the number of Christians in Africa "exploded" in the twentieth century. While barely 9% claimed to be Christian in 1900, 45% (335 million people) claimed to be Christian in 2000.[7] Philip Jenkins estimates the number of Christians in Africa grew from 10 million in 1900 to 360 million in 2000.[8]

Most significant among the African nations experiencing growth are Congo-Zaire, Angola, Swaziland, Zambia, Kenya and Malawi. Christians as percent of the population has mushroomed in one century in Congo-Zaire from 1.4% to 95.4%; in Angola from 0.6% to 94.1%; in Swaziland from 1.0% to 86.9%; in Zambia from 0.3%

to 82.4%; in Kenya from 0.2% to 79.3% and in Malawi from 1.8% to 76.8%.[9]

David Garrison describes the church planting movement among the Massai of Kenya that started with a handful of believers in the early 1980s and now includes more than 15% of the 600,000 Massai tribe. "The worship style of the Maasai is a far cry from the Western forms that marked the colonial era of missions. Most Maasai churches gather under acacia trees, the traditional meeting places for Maasai councils. The Maasai will gather regularly for worship at the same tree again and again. ... The heart of Maasai worship is found in their songs and prayers. The Maasai have an oral culture and have benefited from the telling of Bible stories in their native tongue. Not satisfied to hear the stories told, the Maasai often convert these great teaching stories into their native songs and sing them with great enthusiasm. ... Their Maasai rhythms are hyptnotic as they accompany themselves with the throaty grunts, thumping on chests and things with spears tapping on the floor. Their faces flash vivid expressions as they act out the Bible stories with hand motions and choreographed steps. ... Maasai from Kenya share their faith with the 600,000 Maasai living in Tanzania who are also proving to be responsive. Over the past year, the Maasai evangelists have also begun learning the language of their neighboring tribe, the Samburu people, with a vision of taking the gospel to them."[10]

This amazing and unprecedented growth of the Christian faith across the continent of Africa has not come without a price. At least 1.8 million believers have been martyred in Africa in the twentieth century as a result of their faith in Christ.[11] For instance, while Patrick Johnstone and Jason Mandryk affirm that the Christian population in the Congo (formerly Zaire) has grown from 1.4% in 1900 to over 95% in 2000, they note that "thousands of Christians and hundreds of Catholic and Protestant missionaries were martyred in the Simba Rebellion of 1964."[12]

Asia

My wife and I were visiting Seoul, Korea. On Wednesday morning we woke at 5 a.m. and boarded a bus bound for an early morning prayer meeting at a Presbyterian church. The church conducts prayer meetings every morning at 4 a.m., 5 a.m., 6 a.m. and 7 a.m.. We opted for the 6 a.m. service. When we walked in more than one thousand Korean Christians were quietly sitting in the pews by families. Some were reading their Bibles, some kneeling, others prayed with their heads bowed, their lips whispering prayers reverently. After awhile one of the church leaders stood up and led in worship. It was a moving experience and an introduction into the powerful way that God is working in South Korea and moving across Asia.

With Confucian and Buddhist roots, South Korea has emerged in the last two decades to be the second largest missions sending country in the world. Eighty-nine missionaries were sent from South Korea in 1979. Today the churches in South Korea have more than 12,000 missionaries serving in 160 countries. They are intentionally going to the hardest to evangelize corners of the world, including Iraq, seeking to witness "in a low voice and with wisdom." In June 2004, 33-year-old Kim Sun Il was taken hostage in Baghdad and beheaded. He was sent to Baghdad by the Presbyterain Onnuri Church, a church founded 19 years ago with the specific purpose of training missionaries. The church now has 500 missionaries in 53 countries. Speaking of Kim Sun Il, Mr. Moon of the church's research institute said, "He is a martyr to God's glory. Korean missionaries are eager to do God's work and glorify God. They want to die for God."[13]

The Sarang Community Church in Seoul, Korea has grown to 45,000 members. The church's objective is to "encourage the whole congregation to become world Christians so that they can do domestic and overseas missions as the body of a healthy local church."[14] That one church currently has 127 missionaries around the world and has developed a year-long training program to prepare their people as "lay professional missionaries" who take secular jobs in other nations so they can share Christ with their co-workers and neighbors. They are taking their professions to the ends of the earth. Their Lay Professional Mission states its goal as follows, "Considering the changes in mission circumstances, to be trained as lay professionals and re-equipped as witnesses of the gospel became most important and urgent. The number of nations that limit the official entry of missionaries is increasing. The nations with unreached people groups, which are so called CAN (Creative Access Nations), are reserved for lay professional missionaries." "The 21st century," they conclude, "is the age of the lay professional missionary."[15]

China

David Garrison states that the church is growing faster and that there are more church planting movements in China than any other place on earth. He makes the following observations: "In China more than 30,000 believers are baptized every day. A Church planting movement in a northern Chinese province sees 20,000 new believers and 500 new churches started in less than five years. In Henan province Christianity explodes from less than a million to more than five million in only eight years. Chinese Christians in Qing'an County and Heilongjiang Province plant 236 new churches in a single month. In southern China, a Church planting movement produces more than 90,000 baptized believers in 920 house churches in eight years' time. In 2001 a newly emerging Church planting movement yields 48,000 new believers and 1,700 new churches in one year."[16]

In their book, *Christian Trends*, David Barrett and Todd Johnson take note of the fact that thousands of trained Christians in China are prepared and ready to evangelize the world in the twenty first century.[17]

God has given a vision to the Chinese churches to reach the populations of Asia, the Middle East and Islamic North Africa. Commonly referred to as Back To Jerusalem, it is not a new vision. Its roots grow out of a vision given to Chinese Christians in the 1920s, but it is gaining new momentum. The name is derived from a conviction that God is completing the evangelization of the world that first moved West, circled the globe, and is now moving "back to Jerusalem." Many Chinese believers are convinced that God has given them the task of completing the journey by re-tracing the Silk Road through the strongholds of Hinduism, Buddhism and Islam. They are seeking to penetrate more than fifty countries ranging from North Africa to Southeast Asia. They interpret Back To Jerusalem as "God's call to the Chinese Church to complete the Great Commission."[18]

India

Many think that India is poised for the next great explosion for Christian growth with the potential of eclipsing growth records elsewhere in the world. Doors are opening in India as it rapidly transitions to an industrial and urban nation. India is already a nuclear power and is one of the leading producers of software in the world. Many help desk services for computer software companies in the United States are now located in India.

Philip Jenkins points out that the lowest class in the Hindu caste system, the Dalits, number between 150 and 250 million people, roughly the population of the United States. Jenkins notes that the Dalit population of India equals the total population of Britain, France and Italy combined.[19] Persecuted, outcast and rejected, these poorest of the poor are beginning to turn to Christ.

India is a vast, diverse, multi-cultural and multi-lingual continent. Many people groups are ostracized by the Hindu caste system that dominates India. These groups are responding by forming house churches that multiply in neighborhoods, villages and cities. David Garrison reports that the number of churches among the Kui people in Orissa grew from 200 to more than 1,200 in the 1990s.[20] but such growth is not without cost. In 1999 Graham Staines and his two sons, Philip and Timothy, were attacked while they slept in their station wagon in Manoharpur. Staines had served in India as a missionary since 1965 and was secretary-treasurer of the Evangelical Missionary Society of Mayurbhanj. A mob of about 50 Hindus doused the car with gasoline and set it afire, preventing the victims' escape in retaliation for the large numbers in Manuharpar who have converted to Christ.[21] As has been the case throughout Christian history, the blood of martyrs paves the path to spiritual awakening and revival.

Conclusions

What are we to conclude from this dramatic shift of the Christian center to the Southern Hemisphere? Are we to cease or withdraw from sending missionaries from the North and West? Of course not. If anything, we are to engage the world more dramatically and with greater passion than ever before. God is opening unprecedented doors. More than one and a half billion people still live in countries where more than half the people have never heard the name of Jesus. Most of these live in North Africa, the Middle East, India, East and Southeast Asia. Less than one-third of the world's population claim to be Christian and many of these have a marginal or nominal faith.

We must learn humility and come alongside the indigenous and national leaders God is raising up so that we can join them for collaboration and cooperation. We must realize that some of the most gifted, intelligent and spiritual leaders in the world are emerging from South America, Africa and Asia.

We must collaborate and cooperate with fellow believers around the world for community transformation. Christians in the United

69

States and Europe have access to wealth and resources unavailable in most regions of the world. Millions live in poverty, suffering from unsanitary conditions and malnutrition. Corruption and violence are widespread. We have not yet begun to see what churches, Christian institutions and evangelical organizations can do together working with indigenous leaders around the world to transform communities and nations.

We must realize that we have much to learn from our fellow believers in the South. In particular, the churches of the United States and Europe need to recognize God's supernatural intervention in our day and time. We are in danger of becoming a people who hold the form of religion but deny the power thereof. Our reliance upon corporate and business methods to advance the church has, in many cases, robbed us of the mystery and awe that filled the first century believers and is abundantly present in the churches of the Third World.

We need to learn the importance of discipleship. Churches in the Third World realize new believers need to be discipled since most are coming to Christ from other religions. The West has assumed for too long that new converts automatically know the Bible and the essentials of Christian discipline. In too many churches new converts still receive little more indoctrination than filling out a membership card and standing before a congregation to be welcomed into membership with little or no instruction and no examination.

---

[1] Philip Jenkins, *The Next Christendom, the Coming of Global Christianity*, Oxford University Press, 198 Madison Avenue, NY, NY 10016. pp. 1-2.

[2] Philip Jenkins, *ibid*, pp. 2-3.

[3] CNN.com, March 2, 2001. http://archives.cnn.com/2001/TRAVEL/NEWS/03/02/danger.side/

[4] David Garrison, *Church planting movements*, WIGTake Resources, PO Box 1268, Midlothian, VA 23113. 2004. p. 128.

[5] David Garrison, *ibid.* p. 130.

[6] The Network for Strategic Missions, (http://www.strategicnetwork.org/index.php?loc=kb&view=v&id=6680&fto-983&)

[7] Christian History Institute web site (http://www.gospelcom.net/chi/GLIMPSEF/Glimpses/glmps151.shtml) (Statistical Informatino provided by David Barrett).

[8] Philip Jenkins, *op cit.*p. 4.

[9] Christian History Institute web site, *op cit.*

[10] David Garrison, *ibid.* pp. 89.91.

[11] Christian History Institute. *Ibid.*

[12] Patrick Johnstone and Jason Mandryk, op. cit. p. 198.

[13] Norimitsu Onishi, New York Times, November 1, 2004.

[14] http://worldmission.sarang.org/

[15] *Ibid.*

[16] David Garrison, *ibid.* p. 49.

[17] David Barrett and Todd Johnson, *World Christian Trends*,

[18] Back To Jerusalem web site (http://www.backtojerusalem.com/)

[19] Jenkins, *op cit.*p. 183.

[20] David Garrison, *op cit.* pp. 39-40.

[21] http://www.rediff.com/news/1999/jan/23oris.htm

Questions for Reflection and Discussion

1. How does the information in this chapter change your perspective about missions?

2. What advantages does this shift in the center of Christianity create for missions around the world?

3. What can we learn from our brothers and sisters in Christ in the southern hemisphere?

4. How can your church partner with other churches in other nations for missions?

CHAPTER SEVEN

NEW REALITY #5:
NEW MISSIONS ORGANIZATIONS

In the fall of 2001 all of America and much of the world was recovering from the shock of September 11. Images of the red, silver and blue American Airlines aircraft exploding into the twin towers were still vivid. The choking cloud of dust and debris had scarcely settled over the streets of New York and Washington before the fury of the United States was unleashed on Afghanistan in a swift effort to crush the Taliban and hunt down Osama bin Laden.

Caught in the cross-fire were two young women who had answered God's call to minister to the Afghan people. Recent graduates of Baylor University, Heather Mercer and Dayna Curry were in an Afghanistan prison awaiting a possible death sentence. They had been arrested by the Taliban on August 3 on charges of illegally sharing the gospel in an Afghan home. In the weeks that followed, they sat in their squalid prison cell in Kabul and listened to the bombs of the American advance exploding in the city. Few thought they would survive.

When Kabul fell, the Taliban took their prisoners on their retreat to Kandahar. If they reached Kandahar, their execution was almost certain. But miraculously, on November 13, anti-Taliban forces broke down the prison doors at Ghazni and rescued them.

Dayna Curry and Heather Mercer were not traditional denominational missionaries. They were equipped and sent out by their home church, Antioch Community Church in Waco, Texas. They found their way to Afghanistan through Shelter Now International,

73

a German based ministry that has been providing relief services in Afghanistan and Pakistan for twenty years.

Like Shelter Now, thousands of evangelical entities are springing up providing ways and means for believers to follow God's vision to the ends of the earth. Some are large and well established like Youth With A Mission, Frontiers, Pioneers and Wycliffe International. Most are smaller, barely surviving on month to month donations, but fueled with a passion to carry out God's vision for a world in need.

So, what is new about this? How is this trend different from missions in the twentieth century? To answer these questions we need a little historical perspective on the modern missions movement.

Missions By Societies and Denominations

Most mark the beginning of modern missions with William Carey's departure from England for India in 1793. Prior to that event, post-Reformation Christianity had little or no vision for world missions. The theological battles that produced the fledgling denominations had raged on European soil where Christianity was well established, and, in most places, was the state religion. The debates were not about who would win the lost, or how, but who would control the theological positions and geographical regions. Lutheranism, named for its founder, Martin Luther, dominated Germany and spread to Scandinavia. Presbyterianism was birthed in Geneva by John Calvin. Ulrich Zwingli created the seed bed for Anabaptists in Zurich. Henry VIII broke with Rome over conflict regarding his remarriage to Anne Bolyne and created the Anglican Church in England. The energies of clergy were largely consumed with debates over Scripture interpretation and application. Missions did not surface as a serious concern.

There were exceptions, including the Moravians who sent their first missionaries to the West Indies in 1732. John Wesley, who credited the Moravian missionaries with pointing him toward God's grace, joined George Whitfield to ignite the Great Awakening that swept the American colonies in the early 1700s. But missions as a movement beyond the British Empire and the European theater was little known among Protestants.

In 1792, the young cobbler, William Carey published his pamphlet, *An Inquiry into the Obligation of Christians to Use Means for the Conversion of the Heathen* and shocked his generation. The concept of engaging in efforts to carry the gospel to lands where it had never been preached was virtually inconceivable.

On October 12, 1792, the first Baptist Missionary Society was formed with twelve ministers present. William Carey offered himself as their first missionary. The established clergy of England opposed it. Missions societies continued to form, but they were almost all closely linked to denominations. The Congregationalist Missionary Society formed in 1796 and the Wesleyan Missionary Society (Methodist) formed in 1813. For the next two hundred years, denominations would form the primary base for mission activity.

Methodists credit Thomas Coke as the "Foreign Minister of Methodism." Appointed by John Wesley to work in America, Coke was responsible for extending Wesleyan Missions into the West Indies, parts of England, Wales and Ireland. Fighting against denominational fears that missions would create "foreign entanglements," early Methodist leaders continued to expand their missions outreach. Methodists entered Africa in 1833. By 1925 Methodists had deployed 1,925 missionaries.[1] According to the a recent press release by the United Methodist Church General Board of Global Ministries, UMC now reports a total of 1,069 commissioned and non-commissioned missions personnel.[2]

Presbyterians, tracing their origins to John Calvin of Geneva and John Knox of Scotland, contributed to the Great Awakening in America through such leaders as Jonathan Edwards and Gilbert Tennent. The Pittsburg Presbytery formed the Western Foreign Missionary Society in 1831. The first Presbyterian missionary departed for Liberia in 1833. Like other denominations, Presbyterians divided numerous times in the nineteenth and twentieth century, parts of the divisions occasionally re-uniting. Presbyterian Church in America (PCA), which was organized in 1973, now claims 519 career missionaries in 60 countries along with 169 two-year missionaries and more than 6,500 volunteer missionaries.[3]

The spread of Lutheranism occurred primarily through the migration of German, Norwegian and Scandinavian immigrants who took their faith with them during the first centuries following the Reformation. The Lutheran Church Missouri Synod (LCMS) traces its missionary involvement to 1851. LCMS now reports 275 missionaries including career missionaries, international educators, humanitarian/aid workers and long term volunteers in more than 30 countries. The Department of Global Missions for the Evangelical Lutheran Church of America, ELCA, reports 290 long-term and short-term missions personnel in 47 countries.

Baptists in America first organized for missions in 1814 under the influence of Luther Rice who had returned from India to raise support. It was conflict over missions appointment policies that led to the division of American Baptists in the north and Southern Baptists in the south pre-dating the Civil War. Southern Baptists withdrew and formed their own convention when northern (American) Baptists refused to appoint missionaries who owned slaves.

Southern Baptists adopted a unique approach to missions in 1925 with the creation of the Cooperative Program. Churches were challenged to budget a percentage of their undesignated offerings that could be pooled together for missions support. Churches sent their funds to the local state Baptist conventions. These state conventions adopted budgets for local missions and ministry including a percentage that was forwarded to the Southern Baptist Convention. This percentage varied from state to state. The national body distributed funds with roughly one-half supporting foreign missions, one-fourth supporting home missions and another fourth supporting seminary education.

For almost seventy years the Cooperative Program system worked well with high levels of trust and voluntary sacrifice. Unprecedented millions of dollars of support were created for local, regional, national and international missions efforts. By 1955, Southern Baptists reported 1,000 missionaries under appointment. Under the leadership of Baker James Cauthen, this number grew to 3,000 in 1980. But growing controversy within Southern Baptist ranks starting in the 1980's threatened to derail and dismantle this missions giving system. In spite of the conflicts that have eroded trust at almost every level of Southern Baptist life, the Cooperative Program continues to serve as a significant source for missions support. The International Mission Board reported 5,123 field personnel under appointment in 2004.

The Cooperative Baptist Fellowship (CBF) was formed in 1991 as "a fellowship of Baptist Christians and churches who share a passion for the Great Commission and a commitment to Baptist principles of faith and practice." CBF focuses its Global Missions initiatives "to collaborate with churches and other groups to engage in holistic missions and ministries with the most neglected people in a world without borders." As of 2005, CBF reported 151 Global Missions field personnel.

Early Parachurch Entities

New streams for missions engagement and support began to emerge in the last half of the twentieth century. Parachurch organizations for missions and ministry began to spring up outside denominational structures. These organizations focused on niche ministries and appealed to support from individuals and churches across a wide range of denominational affiliation. By the latter half of the twentieth century, lay believers were beginning to question denominational loyalties. For many, the continued fracturing and splintering of denominations undermined the reasoning that supported the value of one denomination over against all others. Increasingly Christians began searching for the common values of faith that transcended denominational differences and were drawn to emerging parachurch organizations that focused on evangelical essentials while including a broad range of denominational diversity. Christians could find common ground around common goals of evangelism and missions. The Billy Graham Evangelistic Association (BGEA) had enormous influence in this area. Beginning in 1949 and continuing throughout the twentieth century, the BGEA demonstrated in major cities throughout America and around the world that Christians from various denominational traditions could find unity of purpose around the proclamation of the gospel.

The emerging parachurch organizations usually described themselves as non-denominational or interdenominational. Young Life, Campus Crusade for Christ, Youth With a Mission and Wycliffe were among the first.

Young Life was born out of a Presbyterian youth ministry in Gainesville, Texas. Jim Rayburn started by organizing clubs in Gainesville that met in homes with the express purpose of introducing youth to a faith in Jesus Christ that was more about a vibrant relationship than about religion. After graduating from Dallas Seminary, Rayburn officially founded Young Life on October 16, 1941 with its own board of trustees. The clubs spread across Texas by 1946. In 1972, Young Life made a strategic move to reach youth in multi-ethnic and urban settings as well as traditional suburbia. In 2003 Young Life reported 3,200 staff and 16,000 volunteers working in more than 45 countries.[4]

Bill and Vonette Bright started Campus Crusade for Christ in 1951 at UCLA and expanded to forty campuses by 1960. In 1992 Campus Crusade launched its Worldwide Student Network (WSN) to reach students around the world. WSN describes its purpose in this way: "We are committed to building campus movements covering the entire world, movements that are staffed and led by national believers. As visitors, this must be our goal, for nothing less is worth the effort. This means that our desire is to build up national leaders who will eventually replace us as the main working force, not only on the college campuses, but in the community as a whole."[5] The Jesus Film project has become Campus Crusade's most wide-reaching single evangelistic effort. Produced in 1979, the film has been translated into 858 languages and viewed by more than 5 billion people in 228 countries. It has been used by 1,539 denominations and missions agencies.[6] Heather Mercer and Dayna Curry's use of the film in an Afghan home led to their arrest. In 2003 Campus Crusade for Christ International reported 2,900 full-time campus ministry staff.

Youth With A Mission (YWAM) was founded in 1960 by 24-year-old Loren Cunningham. Working out of his bedroom in his parents' home, Cunningham launched YWAM with the single goal of getting youth involved in short term missions where they could make a difference. With remarkable world-wide growth following the small beginning, YWAM began to embrace strategic actions to reach Muslims and other unreached people groups in the 1990s. In 2003, YWAM announced "4k", a concerted effort to reach the neediest parts of the world. YWAM now counts a staff of more than 11,000 and missionaries serving in more than 160 countries on every continent of the globe.[7]

In Guatemala, William Cameron Townsend founded Wycliffe Bible Translators in 1942 after working among the Cakchiquel Indians who wondered why God did not speak their language. In 1934, Townsend organized Camp Wycliffe as a linguistics training school.

By 1942, the "camp" had spawned both Wycliffe Translators and the Summer Institute for Linguistics. The first Bible translation was completed in 1951. Today more than five hundred Bible translations have been completed. Wycliffe works with five thousand active members in more than forty-six countries. Its stated goal is to provide a translation of the Bible into every language group by 2025.[8]

In 1976 Ted Fletcher resigned his position as national sales manager of the Wall Street Journal. Supported by Faith Bible Church in Sterling, Virginia, he and his wife Peggy started Pioneers as a missions agency to connect teams of missionaries and churches for missions. They sent out their first missionary in 1979. Today, Pioneers partners with 1,600 churches to send out more than 1,100 missionaries to the least reached regions of the world. According to their purpose statement, "Pioneers mobilizes teams to glorify God among unreached peoples by initiating church planting movements in partnership with local churches."[9]

Proliferating Entrepreneurial Mission Entities

As the twentieth century drew to a close, the number of missions entities mushroomed. A number of factors contributed to the rapid increase in the number of missions organizations.

(1) **Decline of denominational loyalty**. As Americans became less loyal to brand names, Christians also became less loyal to denominations. Christians who moved to different regions of the country looked for churches that met their spiritual need regardless of denominational affiliation. This created an increasingly fertile field for emerging missions entities that were not connected to any particular denomination.

(2) **Desire for personal involvement**. From the 1960s forward, Americans demonstrated diminishing confidence in large bureaucratic institutions. Increasingly they wanted personal participation.

Decentralization became a movement. The parachurch missions entities offered Christians greater participation and opportunity to connect with individual projects.

(3) **Demand for options and choices.** As Americans demanded more options, so did Christians. Customization became a commodity among consumers and Christians looked for opportunities to customize their choices for missions.

(4) **Development of entrepreneurial initiative.** As entrepreneurial business skyrocketed with new technology and communications power, so did entrepreneurial missions.

 Richard Tiplady, an organizational development consultant in Great Britain, recognizes this trend in his book, *World of Difference, Global Missions At The Pic 'N' Mix Counter.* "We must acknowledge that the mission agency is ceasing to be the only or even the 'normal' means by which individuals become involved in cross-cultural missions. Many other forms of involvement now offer themselves." Young entrepreneurs and former denominational missionaries fueled with a passion for using the tools of the twenty-first century are creating a multitude of options for people to serve Christ to the ends of the earth.

A few examples:

Frontiers is a relative late-comer among the missions entity leaders having been founded in 1982 by Greg Livingstone with the specific purpose of starting churches among Muslim people. Supported by the Evangelical Presbyterian Church, Greg Livingstone served as the North American Director of Arab World Ministries from 1977-1982 before moving to California to launch Frontiers. Today Frontiers has more than 300 missionaries in more than fifty teams and works in over forty countries. Frontiers offers both short term and long term opportunities to serve in Muslim countries.[10]

Word Made Flesh (WMF) was organized in 1991 to serve the poorest of the poor around the world. They partner with local aid organizations, local churches and national believers in India, Nepal, Peru, Romania, Bolivia, Brazil, Thailand and Sierre Leon. Primarily a short term missions entity, WMF organizes Discovery Teams that serve 2-5 weeks and Servant Teams that serve for four months.[11] In a recent issue of "The Cry For Humility," WMF's quarterly publication, Daphne Eck, Director of Advocacy described her experience. She wrote, "This year I celebrated both my thirtieth birthday and my fifth year with WMF. I was 25 years old when I joined WMF – one year older than the average 'Fleshie.' We were all young. The youth of WMF was reflected in our gutsy pioneering efforts among the poor and the freshman attempts at advocacy for the poor. We were a fledgling organization comprised of a few kids with spanking new bachelor's degrees and passion for Jesus and the poor."[12]

Joel Vestal enrolled as a freshman at Baylor University in the early nineties. While a student, God gave him a passion for India and Bangladesh. His web site states, "As a result of walking through the streets of Calcutta, the hospitals of Baghdad, the villages of southeast Africa, the jungles of Indonesia, war torn Sudan, the slums of Cairo, the deserts of Algeria, and oppressed Cuba, it was obvious that an army of indigenous missionaries were eager to evangelize their own people but lacked the training, encouragement, and support ..." As a result Joel started ServLife while a student at Baylor. ServLife now works in twelve nations helping develop indigenous church planters to start indigenous churches that will transform their communities.[13]

Former regional director for World Hunger Relief in Asia, Chip Kingery and his wife Jean established proVISION ASIA in 1986 to provide medical treatment, mobility and job placement so that the handicapped of India can become self supporting. In 1986 they created Ability Connection as a "bridge between community resources and physically challenged individuals." In 1999 they added New Horizon Trust For Disabled to "rehabilitate physically challenged women through vocational training." In 2000 New Vision Braille was established to "assist the visually impaired community programs, job placement and Braille literature." And in 2001 Vision Kraft was created to employ handicapped individuals for full time and part time work. In addition to their focus on the handicapped in India, Jean serves as a corporate trainer for American and Indian businesses.[14]

Shortly after starting WorldconneX, I received a call from Heather Hershap. I listened to her frail voice on my cell phone as she introduced herself. "My name is Heather. I am a student at Truett Seminary. I have cerebral palsy. God has called me to India. How can you help me?"

At about the same time we met Chip Kingery who had founded Pro-VISION ASIA. It seemed too clear a connection to be a coincidence.

After checking references for proVISION ASIA and visiting with Chip to be sure they would be willing to consider working with Heather, I drove to Waco to meet Heather at Truett Seminary. I was immediately impressed. In spite of her wheelchair confinement and the lack of control over her body, Heather radiates a charm few people possess. We visited about her long term goals and dreams, her desire to serve as a counselor to the handicapped and to families dealing with handicap issues.

She told me she had been in church recently and God whispered to her, "India!" For the past couple of weeks, she said she had begun to doubt whether God was really calling her to go to India. "But whenever I begin to doubt," she said, "God gives me a sign." I shared with her the information about proVISION ASIA and watched as her eyes ignited. Pure joy!

Heather and proVISION ASIA immediately connected. But she needed additional help: She needed logistical help for international travel with her limitations. I pondered where we could turn to find help for Heather. Then it dawned on me, sitting by my side in the WorldconneX office was Matt Wallace. We had contracted with Matt to help us with technology issues in our start up. Matt had established his own non-profit corporation called Greater Good Global Support Services (G3S2). I turned to Matt and laid out Heather's request for assistance in international air travel. Matt responded, "That's what we do." G3S2 serves as a 24/7 logistical resource for missionaries and missions anywhere in the world.

It appears Heather will fulfill the dream God gave her to serve the handicapped in India. As of this writing, she is making preparations to serve six weeks in India during the summer of 2005.

Conclusions

So what are we to make out of all of this? First we must recognize the stark reality that the number of missionaries sent out through denominational systems of support is limited. Most denominations are struggling to maintain the number of funded missionaries they currently support and many are cutting back. Denominational missions and missionaries continue to play a significant role in the missions enterprise. These missionaries are still needed. We must pray for them and support them. Denominations continue to offer enormous missions opportunities for short term and career missions.

Second, we must recognize that new and creative missions entities are springing up around the world. Our best estimates indicate there are more than 3,000 missions entities focused on various people groups and ministry needs. Some are quite large and others are small. God is re-wiring the world in the twenty-first century to create unprecedented opportunities for people with entrepreneurial initiative and missional passion to make disciples of all the nations.

For every believer there may be many options available to fulfill God's vision to carry the gospel to the nations of the earth. The day in which we are living is the greatest day for missions in the history of the world. What God desires to do in this generation far exceeds the imagination.

---

[1] http://www.la-umc.org/misshist.htm
[2] http://gbgm-umc.org/global_news/ pr.cfm?articleid=2294&CFID=3377571&CFTOKEN=28616673
[3] http://www.pcanet.org/general/history.htm
[4] http://www.younglife.org
[5] http://r3cru.com/WSN.html
[6] http://www.jesusfilm.org/progress/statistics.html
[7] http://www.ywam.org
[8] http://www.wycliffe.org/wbt-usa/home.htm
[9] http://www.pioneers.org
[10] http://www.frontiers.org/
[11] http://www.wordmadeflesh.com/index.htm
[12] The Cry, And Advocacy Journal of Word Made Flesh, P.O. Box 70 Omaha, NE 68101-0070. Volume 10, No. 4. Winter 2004. p. 2.
[13] http://www.servlife.org/about_vision.html
[14] http://www.provisionasia.org/

Questions for Reflection and Discussion

1. If your church is related to a denomination, how does the denomination engage in missions? Where does the denomination focus its missions efforts?

2. What parachurch/missions entities have you, your church or your family participated with? What kind of missions are these organizations engaged in and where?

3. What missions organizations does your church support?

4. What missions organization would you consider most effective? Why?

CHAPTER EIGHT

NEW REALITY #6:
CHURCHES TO THE FOREFRONT OF MISSIONS

The first-century church at Antioch had no intention of becoming the missions base from which a missions movement would be launched. They were intent on reaching Antioch. Their hands were full with Bible studies conducted in homes throughout the city. The demands required to disciple new believers were overwhelming. The call to missions came as a voice from God. Suddenly, they were catapulted to the front line of missions that would touch the ends of the earth.

Churches sprang up in every direction. Paul planted churches westward into Macedonia, Athens and Rome. Others planted churches in Asia, Bythinia and north Africa, regions Paul never entered. Josephus states that the churches were multiplying so rapidly that no one could count them.

But somewhere the initial dynamic that empowered the first century churches to penetrate the Mediterranean world was lost. Loren Mead, in his book, *The Once and Future Church,* provides the most helpful source I have found in understanding what happened.

Mead divides the missional story of the church into three eras. The first, the Apostolic, extended from the time of Christ to the fourth century. The second, Christendom, extends from the fourth century to the present. We are on the front end of the third era, and what we are now experiencing has more in common with the first century than the twentieth.

The Apostolic Era

The first century churches were spiritual enclaves in a pagan society. Every member was a missionary commissioned to be an agent for transformation by allowing kingdom values to spring from the heart into action. Every Christian was a disciple, a follower of The Way.

The only sending centers for missions were the churches. And, in the Mediterranean world under the Pax Romana, the churches felt themselves connected with the cultures and regions of the known world. Roman commerce and trade made this possible. The long list of language groups assembled in Jerusalem at Pentecost reflects this fact.

There was no central governing body to train, commission and ordain ministers and missionaries. The concept of clergy did not exist. All believers were, in fact and in practice, the "people of God." The decision of the Jerusalem Council in Acts 15 is almost startling in its conclusion to avoid centralization and control. James' letter to the churches makes only minimal demands, and these only as admonitions. Released and empowered, the early church "swarmed" its world and penetrated every strata of society.

The Christendom Era

The establishment of Christianity as the state religion of Rome changed everything. Over time, the Christian faith and the empire became synonymous. The implications for this in regards to missions cannot be overestimated. This moved the missions frontier from the front door to the perimeter of the empire. Everyone within the empire was considered Christian. Everyone outside the empire was considered pagan. It also stole from the individual believer the identity as a missionary in a pagan society. Missions became the province of full-time religious professionals who were sent beyond the boundaries of the empire to penetrate the distant pagan world with the gospel (often extending the empire's culture, since culture and faith were inseparable).

This Christendom paradigm extended beyond the Reformation and gave rise to the practice of colonial missions. In mid-twentieth century America, we considered ourselves a "Christian nation." Our job, as churches and denominations, was to call out the career missionaries who would go for us to the remote places of the earth to preach the gospel. Our task was to study about missionaries, to pray and to give. We would hold the ropes. They would go.

As we have seen in the chapter on the proliferation of missions entities, the nineteenth and twentieth centuries witnessed the emergence of missions efforts by denominations. But local chuches, by and large, did not realize a direct connection with the distant lands and foreign cultures to which the gospel was carried.

Loren Mead states it like this: "… the Christendom paradigm … cut the nerve of personal involvement and responsibility for witness and mission. That personal engagement was replaced with a sense of vicarious participation in a far-off mission carried out by heroes of the faith …"[1]

Denominational structures over the last centuries created a key strength. They provided a means by which churches could pool their resources so that individuals who were called to "go" could do so with confident support. The weaknesses were (1) lack of direct connection between the churches and their missionaries and (2) delegation of personal involvement in finding God's vision for missions and carrying it out.

The Twenty-first Century

Churches are reclaiming their front line position in missions. They are no longer content to "hold the ropes" while others carry the gospel to the ends of the earth. They are no longer content to delegate the responsibility for the appointment and support of missionaries to boards and agencies. They want to go and they want to be personally involved as a congregation in missions. Above all, they want to hear the voice of God.

Richard Tiplady observes, "many local churches are becoming increasingly proactive in their world mission involvement. ... an increasing number of churches are developing their own mission projects without any reference to a mission agency at all."[2]

Missions researchers James Engel and William Dyrness observe, "... local churches have been expected to play only a passive role of support providers. The technological revolution following World War II, however, opened the worldwide door for the local church as never before."[3]

Does this mean that the missions work done by denominations and evangelical entities was wrong? Does this mean there is no place for denominations and missions agencies in the future? Of course not. In many cases the work of denominational and agency missionaries provide the framework for churches to move to the front line. Churches moving to the front line need the wealth of experience and expertise these missionaries can give. Without them, many churches will find their energy and enthusiasm siphoned off into non-strategic and sometimes counter-productive activities. If we refuse to learn from those who have gone before, we are likely to make the same mistakes that have been made before. As churches move to the front line, they must be careful to avoid the arrogance and ignorance of the novice that refuses to listen and learn. They need the cross-cultural training and wisdom for healthy indigenous missions that the more experienced can provide. Missions agencies and entities can play a vital role by helping facilitate the multiplied resources unleashed by the churches.

The pendulum has swung. Churches will not wait. Many are anxious to move beyond praying for missions, giving to missions or even taking an occasional mission trip. They are hungry for strategic missions engagements where God can use them to change the world.

I first met Bob Roberts in the early 1980s. He was pastor of a church with a few hundred in attendance in Southwest Fort Worth. I visited with him to encourage him to start another church to reach the vast numbers of people in his community that his church was not reaching. He flatly refused. To start another church so close to his own would jeapordize the growth and success of his own church.

The next time I heard from Bob a few years later he was a changed person. God had captured his heart and given him a vision for church planting. In fact, he was in the process of starting a new church in Keller, Texas. He invited me to preach for him in the public school where they were meeting.

Since that time, God has expanded Bob Roberts' vision far beyond anything I ever imagined or conceived. Not only has God used him to lead a strong rapidly growing church in Keller and start multiple churches near his own, he has also led his church to embrace Afghanistan and Vietnam for the sake of the Kingdom. God gave him the vision to launch Glocalnet, a network of worldwide churches formed into clusters for the purpose of church multiplication and community transformation. According to the Glocalnet web site, "Glocalnet churches/clusters are committed to three strategic objectives: starting multiplying churches; transforming local communities; impacting the world through nation building."[4]

Glocalnet churches embrace five core values:

"**Strategic partnerships**: We believe we need each other to reach the world! We seek to partner with like-minded churches, as well as other ministries to accomplish our strategic objectives.

Transformational ends: We believer the church of the twenty-first century must make a new kind of disciple, one whose life is characterized by personal transformation. As disciples live transformational lives, we believe that our communities, our cities and our world will be transformed.

Kingdom mindset: We believe that the kingdom of God is much bigger than ourselves! We are more committed to seeing the kingdom extended than we are about our individual church's growth.

Local church driven: We believe that God's design was to use local communities of faith to fulfill the great commission and literally change the world. We pursue these objectives through the local church and through clusters of local churches.

Courage: We believe that authentic disciples of Jesus live counter-cultural lives. We also believe that God calls his church to minister in dangerous places. We courageously seek to live lives that resemble Jesus, and we courageously go to unsafe places as God leads for the sake of the gospel."[5]

This is not just happening in churches who are part of GlocalNet. In some ways, Glocalnet merely reflects the movement of God's spirit in churches on a much larger and broader scale. I met with a group of church planters in Wisconsin in 2003. Each new church pastor stood up and described his vision for his new church. One pastor said, "Our vision is not just to reach our community. Our vision, at the outset, is to start a new church on every continent of the earth." What a great vision and what a great way to start a new church!

In 1987 seven churches from various parts of the United States, representing different denominational and non-denominational traditions, met in Austin Texas to listen to God, to each other and to learn. Their focus was clear: to learn how each one of them could send church planting teams to unreached people groups. It was the beginning of Antioch Network. Antioch Network now supports a full-time staff in Phoenix, Arizona and regional consultants across the United States helping churches network in order to send missions teams.

Sometimes smaller churches wonder where they fit in all of this. What can they do to engage missions at the front line? The answer to that question is difficult if we think only in the old paradigms of raising money to send missionaries. But if we think in the new paradigms of God empowering and releasing His people for missions, it opens up all kinds of possibilities.

I visited with a lay leader in First Baptist Church of Hebron. This little church is over one hundred years old. In 1920 they built a red brick building with stain glass windows on a ridge overlooking the countryside north of Dallas, Texas. The little church stood like a sentry watching the landscape morph from fields of cotton and cattle to a sea of rooftops as the population exploded in the 1980s and 90s. The swelling suburban growth swept past the church like a flood. Landlocked with an acre and a half, the little red brick building remained. Prestonwood Baptist Church, with more than 22,000 members, is located within one-half mile of the Hebron church. Bent Tree Bible Church is almost as close and averages more than 2,000 in attendance. Today, First Baptist Hebron consists of about one hundred people meeting in a little historic red brick building surrounded by people and mega churches.

Jan (not her actual name) joined First Baptist Hebron in 2000 after serving in a Muslim country. Describing her experience, she said, "My church supported me in my decision to return to the Muslim country. However, their financial support was not enough. So, with my last $800 I started a clothing company and became a "tentmaker." It felt like a desperate move at the time, but in hindsight I see it was God's leading. I not only supported myself, but two other full time employees for more than three years. The difference in my ministry was amazing. Suddenly, local friends and acquaintances were relating to me on a more intimate level. I had the same daily struggles with job and money. I had truly become a part of their community. There were so many more opportunities to share Christ because I was working side-by-side with people. I worked hard to earn their respect, and in doing so I earned the right to be listened to." After five years she gave the business to the women she had discipled. At the same time she helped start a new church.

Churches no longer need big budgets and large numbers in order to move to the forefront of missions. How many people are there like Jan in small churches? Like the church at Antioch that separated Paul and Barnabas for the work God gave them, we need to listen to what God is doing in the lives of our people. If we will open our eyes and look, we will discover that God has already brought missions to us! Missions is, indeed, at the door of every church.

To make the leap from the age of Christendom to the missional millennium in the twenty-first century will require a new kind of leadership. Reggie McNeal, a nationally recognized authority on church leadership, agrees with Loren Mead's apostolic references. He states, "In the last decade of the twentieth century, a new leadership genus began appearing on the North American church scene. This leadership is what I and others have dubbed 'apostolic leadership.' This connotation seems appropriate primarily because the challenges to church leaders today parallel those that faced leaders in the first Christian century (commonly called the apostolic era)."[6]

God is not waiting on North America or the West to produce those apostolic leaders. Some of the most gifted apostolic leaders who are opening the way to the future are coming from some of the most unlikely places. But, when we think about it, isn't this consistent with the way God has worked in the past? After all, didn't Jesus emerge from the most unlikely circumstances, and wasn't that the reason many did not recognize Him? He did not fit the pre-conceived patterns for leadership (or Messiahship) in the first century. If we are to recognize what God is doing in our day, we had better prepare ourselves to look in unlikely places to hear and see what God is doing.

Sunday Adelaja was born and raised in a village in Nigeria. He trusted Christ in 1986 and, six months later, accepted a scholarship to study journalism in Byelarussian State university in the USSR. He was planning to return to Nigeria when he says God whispered into his heart, "I have a purpose for bringing you here." His faith was fashioned by perseverance under Communism and by faithfulness following the collapse of the Soviet Union. In 1993, God convinced him to start a new church in Kiev, Ukraine. The vision for the church was clear. He was convinced God wanted him to build a mega church in Kiev. But the vision was not just about Kiev. He was convinced God wanted the church to send out missionaries all over the world, especially to China and to Arab countries.[7]

He started the church in his apartment with seven people. The Embassy of God Church now lists over 20,000 members. The church worships in 20 services every Sunday in various locations in Kiev and has started 100 daughter and satellite churches in the Kiev region. In addition, the church has founded over 200 churches in the former Soviet Union, the United States, Germany,

United Arab Emirates, Holland and Israel.

Many churches are not at the forefront of missions because they consider it too costly, or too risky. They keep their focus on maintaining their buildings and programs rather than sending their people to the ends of the earth. We must constantly re-learn the lesson that the path to survival never leads to the Kingdom. The Kingdom is always discovered down paths of sacrifice and risk.

In recent years we have seen persecution used as an instrument to return the church to the forefront of evangelism and missions. In fact, the Christian faith and churches often thrive under persecution. Land and buildings and budgets, the things we assume to be essential for church growth, are impossible in persecuted circumstances. But, under persecution, the dross of complacency is removed leaving passion, fervor, sacrifice and purity. The pure metal of the Christian faith emerges and the churches become the forefront for evangelism and missions.

It is in the favorable circumstances that the church seems to founder. It becomes obsessed with its buildings, budgets and programs like a mentally unhealthy individual obsessed with diet, health and financial security. The return of the churches to the forefront of missions around the world is the path to health and success. By giving its life away, the church will, in the process, find its life. The words of Jesus are as applicable to churches as they are to individuals. "He who would save his life will lose it. But he who will lose his life for my sake, the same shall save it." The deadliest disease facing any church is survival. Whenever a church (or a Christian organization for that matter) becomes obsessed with survival, its demise is sure. Survival is antithetical to the Christian faith. The path to life is always that path of death and crucifixion. That is why Paul said, "I die daily," (1 Corinthians 15:31) and "I am crucified with Christ, nevertheless I live" (Galatians 2:20). Those words apply to the church as well as to the individual believer.

We are witnessing a re-emergence of New Testament patterns for churches involved in missions in a global context that resembles the first century more than it resembles the twentieth century. The new realities set the stage for churches to reclaim their position at the forefront of missions.

---

[1] Loren Mead, The Once and Future Church, The Alban Institute, Inc. 4125 Nebraska Avenue, NW, Washington, DC 20016, 1991. p. 17.

[2] Richard Tiplady, World of Difference, Global Missions At the Pic 'N' Mix Counter, Paternoster Press, PO Box 1047, Waynesboro, GA, 30830-2047.2003.

[3] James F. Engel, William A Dyrness, Changing the Mind of Missions, InterVarsity Press, P.O. Box 1400, Downers Grove, IL 60515, 2000. pp. 75-76.

[4] http://www.glocal.net/

[5] Ibid.

[6] Reggie McNeal, The Present Future, Jossey Bass, A Wiley Imprint, 989 Market Street, San Francisco, CA 94103-1741, 2003. p 125.

[7] http://www.godembassy.org

Questions for Reflection and Discussion

1. Where is your church directly engaged in missions activity?

2. What is your church doing to minister outside itself in the local community?

3. What is your church doing to minister outside itself in the global context?

4. How can your church encourage and equip members to minister through their careers?

5. Who is God raising up in your church for missions? How can you encourage and assist them?

CHAPTER NINE

NEW REALITY #7:
EMPOWERING THE LAITY

Introduction

When I served as executive director for the Minnesota-Wisconsin Baptist Convention we were faced with a crucial decision regarding one of the traditionally important events on the calendar of most Baptist conventions. The Evangelism Conference for Minnesota-Wisconsin Baptist was no longer effective. It was an enjoyable occasion for friendship and fellowship. But it wasn't making any significant difference in our churches or their effectiveness in their communities. It was, by its very nature, a "clergy" event: preachers visiting with preachers talking preacher talk.

We became convinced the event needed to be completely rede-signed. If the churches were to be energized and empowered for effective ministry, we needed to reach the laity. We formed a steering committee composed primarily of laity. We gave them a blank sheet of paper and challenged them to design a "Congress of the Laity."

The first thing they did was to reject our name for the new event. They weren't comfortable with anything that smacked of "con-gress." They chose the name "Empower." They structured the event to include creative ministries led by laity in the churches and enlisted gifted lay leaders - both men and women - to challenge, teach and equip those who assembled. They designed it as a family event so all ages could participate. They planned break out confer-ences for special interests that would meet the needs of church members. They recruited the most gifted and creative worship leaders in the churches and turned the worship experience over to them. The attendance zoomed from 160 to more than 800. Since we had only 120 pastors, we knew we were reaching the laity.

But a surprising thing happened. When we began to challenge the churches to empower their church members by giving them permission, encouragement and support to follow their passions for ministry, lay people began coming up to me weeping. They would tell me of a passion they had for a particular ministry only to have their dream referred to a committee where it was squelched and died. Too often their ministry passions did not fit the traditional programs that were expected to create larger attendance and increased budget for the church. While some pastors applauded what God was doing among the laity and made the adjustments in their churches, others viewed these creative members as a threat to their authority.

We were experiencing an early expression of what is continuing to gain momentum. The laity are no longer content to take up the offering, sit on the pew, populate the programs and do what they are told. They want to be involved. They want their rightful place in the Kingdom movement of the people of God. And, in many instances, they want to go to the ends of the earth with their professions and their passions. God was teaching us to ask new questions. Most churches looked at new members and asked, "What can you do for our church?" Others began to ask, "What is God's dream for your life? How can we help you fulfill God's dream?" These churches began to be fueled by new dreams and visions. New energy and creativity was released. Churches that made the change began to move beyond program and organization to dynamic and innovative ministry.

Laity in the First Century

The concept of laity and clergy would have been inconceivable to the first century believers. There was only one "class" of believers: disciples. The only term Jesus consistently used for those who chose to follow Him was "disciple." "Disciple" remained the most used term to identify followers of Christ in the early church. The term disciple or disciples is used 272 times in the New Testament. Occasionally believers are referred to as those of "the Way," (Acts 9:2; 19:23; 22:4; 24:14,22) or those who "believe in the Name." Not until Antioch were believers referred to as "Christians" (Acts 11:26). The term Christian occurs only two other times in the Bible (Acts 26:28; 1 Peter 4:16).

That every believer was considered a disciple indicates there was no hierarchy of commitment or devotion within the body of Christ. There were, of course different roles for service within the body of Christ: apostles (*apostoloi)*, bishops (*episkopoi*), elders (*presbuteroi*), deacons (*diakonoi*) and pastors (*poimonoi*), but these are not clearly defined and distinct offices. They indicate roles of service for equipping and teaching to nurture the faith and practice of believers. The term for laity comes from the Greek word *laos* which is translated "people." We are all the "people" of God. This is the term that Peter used in 1 Peter 2:9-10:

> "But you are a chosen race, a royal priesthood, a holy nation, a people (*laos*) for God's own possession, so that you may proclaim the excellencies of Him who has called you out of darkness into His marvelous light. For you once were not a people (*laos*), but now you are the people (*laos*) of God; you had not received mercy, but now you have received mercy."

In our vocabulary the term "layman" or "lay person" carries the connotation of an amateur. Webster's defines a layman as a "person not belonging to or skilled in a given profession." Conse-

101

quently, when I visit my doctor and want him to give me a diagnosis I can understand, I ask him to put it in "layman's terms." This is the definition most Christians have in mind when they think of themselves as "laity." They consider themselves unskilled and not belonging to the profession of the "clergy" who are the religious professionals.

Nothing could be further from the New Testament's description of believers in Jesus Christ. The religious professionals were the Jewish Scribes and the Pharisees. The disciples were fishermen, tax collectors and common laborers. There were no religious professionals and there were no amateurs among the ranks of Christian disciples.

Pentecost marked the fulfillment and the beginning of God's activity among men. It was the fulfillment because Jesus clearly taught that this was the reason he was going away: "But I tell you the truth, it is to your advantage that I go away; for if I do not go away, the Helper shall not come to you; but if I go, I will send him to you." (John 16:7). It was also the beginning, because the Holy Spirit would work in the lives of Jesus' followers in ways that had not been possible before: "But when He, the Spirit of truth comes, He will guide you into all the truth; for He will not speak on His own initiative, but whatever He hears, He will speak; and He will disclose to you what is to come. He shall glorify Me; for He shall take of Mine, and shall disclose it to you." (John 16:13-14).

This initial outpouring of the Holy Spirit was pure. **The Helper gave all of God's word to all of God's people, (young and old, men and women) to do all of God's work.** As a result, three thousand were baptized that day in Jerusalem.

But the Spirit's work on the earth was soon in jeopardy. The rapid growth of the church at Jerusalem was in danger of turning inward. It was the first, but by far not the last, effort of the Adversary to abort the missionary nature of the Holy Spirit's work in the church. The rushing roar as a mighty wind that character-ized the birth of God's spirit in the hearts of men at Pentecost was replaced by a murmuring of complaint among the members. The Greek-speaking members were complaining that their widows were not getting as much attention as the Jewish widows in the daily distribution of food.

The twelve met to discuss the problem and work on a solution. They considered two alternatives. They could get up earlier, stay up later, and concentrate on making sure the Greek speaking widows were not neglected. Or, they could turn the problem over to the larger body of believers, include the congregation in the solution and empower the "laity" to minister to one another. They chose the latter (Acts 6:1-4).

This made all the difference. Instead of vesting authority and responsibility in a few who could minister to the many, they would include the whole body of believers in ministry. As a result, God continued to give all of His Word to all of His people.

Luke illustrated this by documenting the activities of Stephen and Philip, two of the men chosen by the congregation to lead out in ministry. We would expect Luke to concentrate on how Stephen and Philip carried out their task of caring for the Greek speaking widows and how the complaining subsided. Instead, Acts 7-8 focuses on how these two men gave leadership for the proclama-tion and dissemination of the *kerygma*, the essential gospel of Jesus Christ.

The Holy Spirit immediately authenticated Stephen's ministry with signs and wonders. As a result, he was dragged before the Council of the High Priest and accused of seeking to destroy the temple and undermine their Jewish customs. To this charge, Stephen gave an eloquent summary of God's redemptive work starting with Abraham and concluding with Jesus' death, burial and resurrection. Clearly, Stephen is an example that when God sent His Holy Spirit

He gave all of His Word to His people.

The hostile response to Stephen's courageous stand resulted not only in Stephen's death, cheered on by a young Pharisee named Saul, it launched a wide-spread persecution of Jesus' followers in Jerusalem. "And on that day a great persecution arose against the church in Jerusalem; and they were all scattered throughout the regions of Judea and Samaria, **except the apostles.**" (Acts 8:1)

The only ones who did not leave Jerusalem were the leaders. The general populace of believers, men and women, young and old, fled to the remote regions of Judea and Samaria. And what did they do? "Therefore, those who had been scattered went about preaching the word." (Acts 8:4). All the people of God began to carry the Word of God to the whole world.

The remainder of Acts 8 picks up on the experiences of Philip, another of the seven men chosen to "serve tables" in Acts 6. Philip immediately began proclaiming Christ in Samaria. That God chose to give Philip, and others, both His Word and His work is indicated by the fact that the people "heard and **saw the signs** he was performing." (Acts 8:6). As with Jesus and with the seventy of Luke 10, unclean spirits were obedient to the name of Jesus. The paralyzed and lame began to walk.

This, of course, was not the first time the Samaritans had heard of Jesus. They had, in fact, met him months earlier when God's chosen evangelist on that occasion was an adulterous woman. (John 4). Philip merely told them the rest of the story: the crucifixion, burial, resurrection and ascension of Jesus.

Their response was immediate. The apostles who were still in Jerusalem sent Peter and John to check it out. It is important to note that the apostles were not the vanguard but the rear guard for the Samaritan movement. God's people were on the front line.

To underscore this point, Luke follows Philip to the desert road that connects Jerusalem and Gaza. Here he encountered the treasurer of Ethiopia returning to his own country after worshipping in Jerusalem. He was reading Isaiah 53, the suffering servant prophecy. Confused about the meaning of this passage, he invited Philip to join him and heard for the first time about Jesus. He was immediately baptized by this itinerant layman.

If the book of Acts is about the expansion of the gospel across national and cultural barriers to the ends of the earth, Luke has made it abundantly clear that the means God chose to accomplish this was the laity. So much so that the young Pharisee, Saul, was dispatched to stamp out the growing movement of Jesus' followers in Damascus, a journey that would change his life and the record of the Christian movement forever.

This pattern continues throughout Acts: God's Word and God's work were given to all of His people to reach the whole world. We find evidence at Antioch in the home of Nicholas, another of the seven men selected in Acts 6. It was in Antioch that the church took on its first true multi-ethnic dimension. The believers, who were called Christians here for the first time, took under their wing the novice, Saul, and, after mentoring him, sent him out with Barnabas on the first missionary journey.

Wherever churches were planted, the laity became leaders. At Antioch of Pisidia, Lystra, Iconium and Derbe, they looked for converts with a good reputation in the community and in the church, for those who were wise and good stewards of their own finances and their own families. These they appointed as leaders in the churches(Acts 14:23). The trend continued in Philippi, Thessalonica, Berea, Athens, Corinth, Ephesus and countless other unnamed places stretching into Asia and Africa. Paul later passed on these instructions to his young protégés Timothy and Titus (Titus 1:5-9; 1 Timothy 3:1-13). By using this method, the gospel penetrated the Mediterranean world within two hundred years.

Laity and Clergy

So where did the whole idea of clergy and laity come from? Kenneth Scott Latourette has long been recognized as one of the paramount authorities in Christian history. According to Dr. Latourette, "As early as the beginning of the second century a distinct cleavage had begun to appear between clergy and laity ... By the end of the second century the clergy had clearly become a separate 'order,' that designation having probably been derived from the designation given to Roman magistrates in a tightly stratified society."[1]

The distinction between clergy and laity with a privileged class of priests who were given special spiritual authority became crystallized in the Roman Catholic system. The church became the sole authority for matters of faith and practice and the interpretations by popes and priests were final. "Laity," as unskilled and uninformed amateurs in spiritual things, could not be trusted with Scripture or theology. The eternal destiny of the laity and the treasures of salvation were firmly placed in the hands of the priests. Even governments bowed in submission to the powerful positions of pope and priests as the Catholic religion swept Europe during the Middle Ages.

The Reformation corrected much of this. Scripture was again placed in the hands of the people and the gospel of salvation by faith in Jesus Christ alone was once again proclaimed. But the concept of clergy and laity remained. The great divide continued.

Following the Reformation, Mead contends, "the shattered Christendom paradigm produced denominational shards, each of which perpetuated something of the paradigm within its own boundaries. There was a make-believe quality in each shard's assumption that its world was a microcosm of the whole world of which it was the remnant, as if nothing else exists."[2]

The nineteenth and twentieth centuries, the age of denominations, became the age of the professional missionary. Missions education systems for denominations focused on teaching about missionaries, calling people to pray for missionaries and encouraging people to give in order to support missionaries. They did not focus on teaching missions.

Laity in the Twenty-first Century

Here is an interesting question. Can a lay person be a missionary? Traditionally we have thought of missionaries as those who are ordained and seminary trained. But is this accurate or adequate? The Bible does not use the term missionary. The term Jesus preferred for all of his followers was "disciple." The only relevant question is, "Are you a disciple of Jesus Christ?" According to what Jesus taught, every disciple is a missionary.

Increasingly lay people want to become personally engaged in missions and they are often willing to make significant sacrifice to do so. Kenneth Eldred expressed the desire of many lay people. "As a new believer, I wanted to be a Christian full-time, not just a week-end warrior whose faith had no bearing on his weekday activities. Slowly I began to understand what that meant. God began teaching me how to bring the two parts together."[3]

This first came into focus for me in the early 1990s. I had been serving as interim pastor for the First Baptist Church of Lewisville, Texas. The church had taken a number of significant steps forward during the interim including purchase of land where they would eventually relocate and more than triple in attendance. In January 1993, I announced to the church that God was leading me to leave my native state of Texas and move my family north to lead the Minnesota-Wisconsin Baptist Convention.

When I did so, Jim and Marion Wiersema stopped me in the hallway of the church. They had been members of the church for a number of years, but Jim had recently been laid off as an employee at General Dynamics in Fort Worth. Something I said about God's call upon our lives to relocate to Minnesota-Wisconsin resonated with Jim and Marion. "When you get to Minnesota, if you find something I can do, let me know," Jim spoke with a wry smile. "I can be just as unemployed in Minnesota or Wisconsin as I am in Texas."

Not long afterward I called Jim about a new church starting in Oshkosh, Wisconsin that needed help. That summer Jim and Marion left their children and grandchildren behind, moved to Oshkosh and went to work. They took odd jobs for support, encouraged the church and organized an outreach to the Oshkosh Fly-In, the largest annual event in the nation for private pilots.

Over the next several years Jim and Marion would help a number of churches in Wisconsin. Jim often served as a lay interim pastor and helped churches "re-dream" their dream. In 2002, the North American Mission Board chose Jim and Marion from more than 2,000 volunteers as the Mission Service Corps couple of the year. Marion passed away from cancer in 2004. Jim continued to serve in Wisconsin.

While Jim and Marion did not leave the United States to work overseas, they did pull up roots and relocate 1,200 miles from home in a different culture and climate (including sub-zero winters) in order to fulfill God's call for their lives. Other men and women are making similar moves and sacrifices to follow God.

Unfortunately the clergy-laity dichotomy in our western culture leads both laity and church leadership to assume that a person has to make a choice between business and church if they are going to be engaged in missions. Only a few are yet considering the possibility that they could take their gifts for successful business and use them to carry the gospel to the ends of the earth.

Here are a couple of examples of laity who are discovering how God wants to use them in their professions:

Peter Tsukahira describes himself as an Asian-American Israeli. He looks Asian, speaks American English and now lives on Mount Carmel in Israel. He was born in Boston and married Rita, who is from a Jewish family. Peter and Rita became believers in Jesus Christ in the early 70s. Like many others, Peter picked up computer programming for software in the 1970s in California in an era when the market for PCs and software was just taking off. They began to look for open doors to serve in Japan. Peter says, "Rather than raise support money from different congregations, however, I realized that I had a valuable asset in my computer knowledge. I had worked in the industry for five years and had experience in a number of different departments. So I sent my resume to about ten Japanese companies."[4] In 1981 he moved to Tokyo with NEC Corporation and invested his life in the growth of an international congregation that grew to more than 200. Peter accepted no salary while serving as pastor of the congregation. In 1987 Peter and Rita moved to Israel where they are giving leadership to groups of messianic Jews.

I attended a conference at the Harley Davidson Motorcycle factory in Kansas City in 2002. We met with the executives and managers who led Harley Davidson from near bankruptcy in the mid 1980's to one of the most successful businesses in the United States. One of their young executives had successfully launched the Buell sport bike in Europe. He introduced himself by saying, "I am a disciple of Jesus Christ disguised as an executive of Harley Davidson."

Many believe that we are on the verge of the next great missions movement in history. Imagine the enormous possibilities if businessmen and professionals were to see their business and their professions as the means by which God will use them to carry the Gospel to the ends of the earth. If the church continues to rely upon "professional missionaries" with seminary degrees and denominational credentials to reach the world, the church's impact on the world will remain stunted. We are in effect attempting to force the enormous power and almost unlimited resources of the church through a narrow bottleneck. Releasing and empowering the laity to use their entrepreneurial gifts to start businesses worldwide where Christians can saturate societies with authentic discipleship would create an evangelistic wave more powerful than the 2004 tsunami in Southeast Asia.

Where does this leave the clergy? Are the clergy unnecessary to the Kingdom enterprise of God? Of course not. While the concept of "clergy" is not present in the New Testament, the need for gifted believers who can equip others is quite clear. That is why churches will always need pastors and teachers. Their effectiveness is measured by the extent to which they equip and empower all the people of God to be disciples of Jesus Christ who carry the gospel to the ends of the earth (Ephesians 4:11-12).

---

[1] Kenneth Scott Latourette, A History of Christianity, New York, Harper and Brothers, 1953. p. 133.

[2] Ibid. p. 18

[3] Kenneth A. Eldred, "Kingdom Based Investing," On Kingdom Business, Tetsunao Yamamori and Kenneth A. Eldred Editors, *On Kingdom Business, Transforming Missions Through Entrepreneurial Strategies*. Crossway Books, A Division of Good News Publishers, 1300 Crescent Street, Wheaton, Illinois 60187. 2003,

[4] Peter Tsukahira, "The Integration of Business and Ministry" Ibid. p. 120.

Questions for Reflection and Discussion

1. According to the Bible, what can clergy do in Christian life and ministry that laity cannot do?

2. What are the qualifications to be a missionary?

3. What activity in your Christian life causes you to feel God's pleasure?

4. If you could do anything you wanted to do as a Christian to serve God and others, what would it be? What is your dream?

5. How could your business create a base for missions?

FOR FURTHER READING

James F. Engel, William A Dyrness, *Changing the Mind of Missions,* InterVarsity Press, P.O. Box 1400, Downers Grove, IL 60515, 2000.

David Garrison, *Church planting movements,* WIGTake Resources, PO Box 1268, Midlothian, VA 23113. 2004.

Darell Guder, *Missional Church, A Vision for the Sending of the Church in North America,* Wm. B. Eerdmans Publishing Co., 255 Jefferson Ave. SE, Grand Rapids, MI 49503. 1998.

Reggie McNeal, *The Present Future,* Jossey Bass, A Wiley Imprint, 989 Market Street, San Francisco, CA 94103-1741, 2003.

Loren Mead, *The Once and Future Church,* The Alban Institute, Inc. 4125 Nebraska Avenue, NW, Washington, DC 20016, 1991

Milfred Minatrea, *Shaped By God's Heart,* Josey Bass, 989 Market Street, San Francisco, CA, 94103-1741, 2004.

Philip Jenkins, *The Next Christendom, the Coming of Global Christianity,* Oxford University Press, 198 Madison Avenue, NY, NY 10016,2002.

Patrick Johnstone and Json Mandruk, *Operation World,* Paternoster Publishing PO Box 1047, Waynesboro GA 30830-2047, 2001

Steve Rundle and Tom Steffen, *Great Commission Companies,* InterVarsity Press, P.O. box 1400, Downers Grove, IL 60515-1426, 2003.

Patrick Johnstone, *The Church Is Bigger Than You Think,* William Carey Library Publishers, P.O. Box 40129, Pasadena, CA 91104, 1998.

Tetsunao Yamamori and Kenneth A. Eldred, editors, *On Kingdom Business, Transforming Missions Through Entrepreneurial Strategies.* Crossway Books, A Division of Good News Publishers, 1300 Crescent Street, Wheaton, IL 60187, 2003.

ABOUT THE AUTHOR

William (Bill) Tinsley serves as Leader for WorldconneX Mission Network, a new missions entity created by the Baptist General Convention of Texas in 2004 to connect God's people for God's vision. He has served as founding pastor for four churches, Director of Missions for Denton Baptist Association, Denton, Texas; Executive Director of the Minnesota-Wisconsin Baptist Convention and Associate Executive Director of the Baptist General Convention of Texas. He has led missions conferences in Australia, New Zealand, Brazil, Russia and Guatemala.

BOOKS BY WILLIAM TINSLEY

Upon This Rock, Dimensions of Church Planting 1986

Breaking the Mold, Church Planting in the Twenty-first Century 1996

The Jesus Encounter, Stories of People In the Bible Who Met Jesus 2001

Authentic Disciple, Meditations in Mark 2003

To Order Books by William Tinsley
Go To: www.veritaspublish.com